THE ULTIMATE CHALLENGE

THE ULTIMATE CHALLENGE

B🌾XTREE

First published 2000 by Boxtree
an imprint of Macmillan Publishers Ltd
25 Eccleston Place
London SW1W 9NF
Basingstoke and Oxford

Associated companies throughout the world

www.macmillan.co.uk

ISBN 0 7522 7191 1

Produced under licence from Celador Productions Limited
Copyright © 2000 Celador Productions Limited

9 8

A CIP catalogue record for this book
is available from the British Library.

Designed and typeset by Blackjacks
Printed by Mackays of Chatham plc

CONTENTS

How to play

If you scratched your head and chewed your nails over the teasers in *Who Wants To Be A Millionaire? The Quiz Book*, then brace yourselves because *The Ultimate Challenge* is sure to test you to your absolute limits! It's a little trickier this time because before you can make your stake for the £1,000,000, you must earn your place in the hot-seat by making it through the Fastest Finger First round. You can make it personal and challenge yourself, or invite some friends round and see who's got the brawniest brain!

FOR 1 PLAYER

As on *Who Wants To Be A Millionaire?*, the aim of the game is to reach £1,000,000. Before you can even think about the cash, you must first correctly answer a question from the Fastest Finger First section. You have just 30 seconds to put the letters in the correct order. When time's up, follow the page reference at the foot of the page to find out if you can take your place in the hot-seat and begin your climb for the cash!

Once in the hot-seat

Start with a question worth £100 and once you have decided on your final answer (and you are absolutely sure ...) follow the page reference at the foot of the page to find out if you've won that amount. If your answer is correct, you can play to win £200 and so on up the tree. The page where each money level begins is listed in the answer section.

As on the programme you have three lifelines to help you on your way to £1,000,000. These are, of course, optional but each of them can only be used once, so only use them when you really need to.

Fifty-Fifty

This option takes away two incorrect answers leaving the correct answer and one incorrect answer remaining, a page reference at the bottom of each page will direct you to the relevant section.

Ask the Audience

This works in exactly the same way as on *Who Wants To Be A Millionaire?* except we've asked the audience so you don't have to! Simply follow the page reference at the bottom of each page to find out what the audience thought. In the end, however, the final decision is yours.

Phone a Friend

If you have a telephone handy (and a willing friend!) ring him/her up to help you out. You have thirty seconds (no cheating, now ...) to read the question to your friend and for them to tell you what they think the answer is. If there's someone else around, ask if they can time it for you.

If you answer incorrectly, you are out of the game. £1,000 and £32,000 are 'safe havens' so if you answer a question incorrectly and you have not reached £1,000 then not only are you out of the game but you won't have won a penny! If you have reached one (or both) of these havens and you answer a question incorrectly, then you are out of the game but you will have won the value of the previous haven you have reached. If at any point during the game you are unsure of an answer and don't want to risk being out of the game if you answer incorrectly, you can 'stick' at the amount you have won so far and that will be your final score. As you play, use the score sheets at the back of the book to keep a running record of the amount you have won and the lifelines you have used.

FOR 2–5 PLAYERS

Players should take it in turns at being 'Chris Tarrant' and posing questions to the other contestant/s. The rules are the same as for a single player (see pages 6–7). If someone reaches £1,000,000, that person is the winner and the game is over. Otherwise, whoever has won the most money when everyone else is out is the winner.

Are you ready to play? Good. With all that money at stake, we're sure we don't need to tell you to think very carefully before you give your final answer. Good luck and be sure to remember at all times the motto of *Who Wants To Be A Millionaire?* – it's only easy if you know the answer!

FASTEST FINGER FIRST

FASTEST FINGER FIRST

1

Starting at the rod end, put these items on a standard fishing line in order.

A: Float

B: Reel

C: Fly

D: Line

2

Starting with the longest, put these sports in order of distance from net top to playing surface.

A: Volleyball

B: Table tennis

C: Lawn tennis

D: Netball

3

Put these countries in chronological order according to when they joined the European Union.

A: United Kingdom

B: Finland

C: Greece

D: France

4

Starting with the most, put these months in order according to how many days were in each.

A: July 1999

B: February 1999

C: June 1999

D: February 2000

5

Starting in 1901, put these royal consorts in order according to when their spouses reigned in Britain.

A: Elizabeth

B: Mary

C: Philip

D: Alexandra

Turn to the answer section on page 269 to see if you've earned a place in the hot seat!

FASTEST FINGER FIRST

6

Starting with the earliest, put these events in order according to when they usually occur during a year.

- A: Wimbledon Championships
- B: FA Cup Final
- C: Cowes Week
- D: Grand National

7

Starting nearest London, put these cities in their order along the M4 from east to west.

- A: Swansea
- B: Bath
- C: Bristol
- D: Cardiff

8

Starting in January, put the seasons in order according to when they occur in Australia.

- A: Autumn
- B: Spring
- C: Summer
- D: Winter

9

Starting with the longest, put these musical notes in order, according to their time value.

- A: Minim
- B: Crotchet
- C: Quaver
- D: Semibreve

10

Starting with the least number of years, put these wedding anniversaries in order.

- A: Coral
- B: Lace
- C: Paper
- D: Silver

Turn to the answer section on page 269 to see if you've earned a place in the hot seat!

FASTEST FINGER FIRST

11

Starting from the 1940s, put these people in the order they managed Manchester United.

A: Ron Atkinson

B: Tommy Docherty

C: Alex Ferguson

D: Matt Busby

12

Starting with the earliest, put these hits in the order they were UK number one singles for Elton John.

A: Don't Let The Sun Go Down On Me

B: Don't Go Breaking My Heart

C: Candle in the Wind

D: Sacrifice

13

Starting with the earliest, put these statesmen of ancient Rome in chronological order.

A: Romulus

B: Hadrian

C: Julius Caesar

D: Constantine

14

Starting with the smallest, put these prefixes in order according to the number they denote.

A: Quadri-

B: Deca-

C: Octo-

D: Quint-

15

Starting with the first, put the four Christian names of Prince William's father in alphabetical order.

A: Charles

B: Philip

C: Arthur

D: George

Turn to the answer section on page 269 to see if you've earned a place in the hot seat!

FASTEST FINGER FIRST

16

Starting with the shortest, put these periods of time in order according to how many years are in each.

A: Olympiad

B: Bicentenary

C: Decade

D: Millennium

17

Starting with the fewest, put these solid shapes in order according to how many surfaces each has.

A: Cone

B: Cube

C: Cylinder

D: Sphere

18

Starting with the earliest, put these scientists in the order they were born.

A: Isaac Newton

B: Galileo Galilei

C: Albert Einstein

D: Stephen Hawking

19

Put these four television presenters in alphabetical order of their surnames.

A: Jonathan Dimbleby

B: Julia Somerville

C: Jeremy Paxman

D: Judy Finnigan

20

Starting with the earliest, put these children's characters in the order they were created.

A: Harry Potter

B: Charlie Bucket

C: Ratty and Mole

D: Mad Hatter

Turn to the answer section on page 269 to see if you've earned a place in the hot seat!

FASTEST FINGER FIRST

21

Put these European countries
in order from north to south.

A: Denmark
B: Finland
C: France
D: Greece

22

Put these Wimbledon singles champions
in the order they first won the title.

A: Boris Becker
B: Pete Sampras
C: John McEnroe
D: Rod Laver

23

Starting with the longest, put these lengths in order.

A: Micrometre
B: Centimetre
C: Decimetre
D: Millimetre

24

Put the four seasons in alphabetical order.

A: Spring
B: Summer
C: Autumn
D: Winter

25

Put these words in the order
they appear in a popular proverb.

A: Hand
B: Worth
C: Bird
D: Bush

Turn to the answer section on page 269 to see if you've earned a place in the hot seat!

FASTEST FINGER FIRST

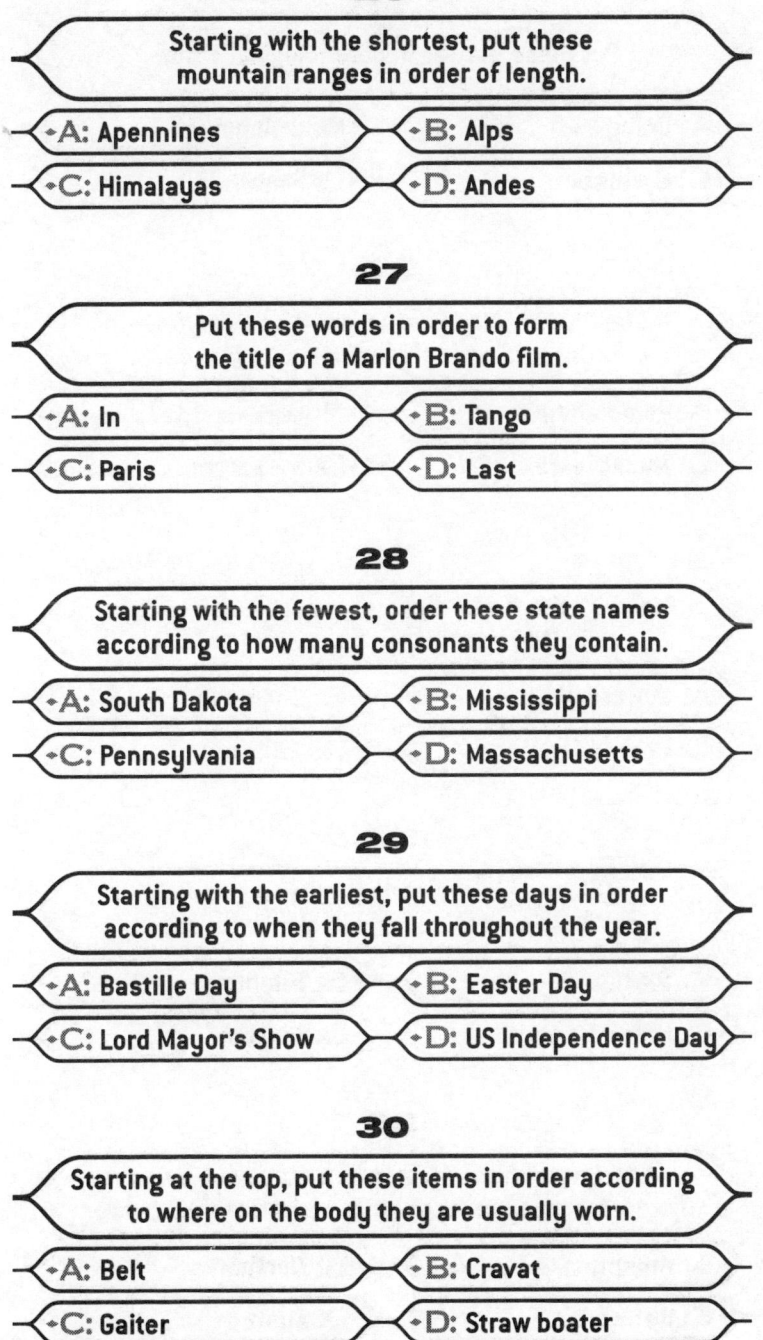

26

Starting with the shortest, put these mountain ranges in order of length.

A: Apennines
B: Alps
C: Himalayas
D: Andes

27

Put these words in order to form the title of a Marlon Brando film.

A: In
B: Tango
C: Paris
D: Last

28

Starting with the fewest, order these state names according to how many consonants they contain.

A: South Dakota
B: Mississippi
C: Pennsylvania
D: Massachusetts

29

Starting with the earliest, put these days in order according to when they fall throughout the year.

A: Bastille Day
B: Easter Day
C: Lord Mayor's Show
D: US Independence Day

30

Starting at the top, put these items in order according to where on the body they are usually worn.

A: Belt
B: Cravat
C: Gaiter
D: Straw boater

Turn to the answer section on page 269 to see if you've earned a place in the hot seat!

FASTEST FINGER FIRST

31

Put these battles in chronological order.

A: Crécy | B: El Alamein

C: Gettysburg | D: Marathon

32

Starting with the fewest, put these groups in order according to the usual number in each.

A: Commandments | B: Horsemen of the Apocalypse

C: Musketeers | D: Wonders of the Ancient World

33

Starting with the earliest, put these English kings in the order in which they reigned.

A: Edward IV | B: George IV

C: Henry IV | D: William IV

34

Starting in the northeast of England, put these coastal resorts in clockwise order.

A: Blackpool | B: Brighton

C: Great Yarmouth | D: Scarborough

35

Starting with the most, place these countries in order by the number of other countries they border.

A: Argentina | B: Denmark

C: Germany | D: Mexico

Turn to the answer section on page 269 to see if you've earned a place in the hot seat!

FASTEST FINGER FIRST

36

Starting with the earliest, put these actresses in order according to when they first won an Oscar.

- A: Shirley Booth
- B: Luise Rainer
- C: Frances McDormand
- D: Louise Fletcher

37

Starting with the earliest, put these four footballers in order according to the year of their birth.

- A: George Best
- B: Gary Lineker
- C: Stanley Matthews
- D: Michael Owen

38

Starting with the earliest, put these four US presidents in the order they became head of state.

- A: Thomas Jefferson
- B: Abraham Lincoln
- C: William McKinley
- D: George Washington

39

Starting with the earliest, put these composers in the order they died.

- A: Berlioz
- B: Elgar
- C: Mozart
- D: Verdi

40

Starting with the earliest, put these famous buildings in the order they were established.

- A: Millennium Dome
- B: Statue of Liberty
- C: Sydney Opera House
- D: Wembley Stadium

Turn to the answer section on page 269 to see if you've earned a place in the hot seat!

FASTEST FINGER FIRST

41

Starting with the earliest, put these four feline films in chronological order of their first release.

- A: The Aristocats
- B: Cat Ballou
- C: Cat on a Hot Tin Roof
- D: Octopussy

42

Starting with the earliest, put these Winter Olympic venues in chronological order.

- A: Albertville
- B: Calgary
- C: Lillehammer
- D: Nagano

43

Starting with the mythological creature, put these Chinese animal years in their correct order.

- A: Dog
- B: Monkey
- C: Horse
- D: Dragon

44

Starting with the earliest, put these historic events in chronological order.

- A: Boston Tea Party
- B: First Man on Moon
- C: Outbreak of Korean War
- D: Death of Abraham Lincoln

45

Put the Queen Mother's name at birth in the correct order.

- A: Elizabeth
- B: Angela
- C: Marguerite
- D: Bowes-Lyon

Turn to the answer section on page 269 to see if you've earned a place in the hot seat!

FASTEST FINGER FIRST

46

Starting with the furthest north, put these American states on the Atlantic coast in order.

- A: South Carolina
- B: New Jersey
- C: Maine
- D: North Carolina

47

Put these words in order to form the title of a famous musical.

- A: Get
- B: Your
- C: Annie
- D: Gun

48

Starting with the least number of years, put these wedding anniversaries in order.

- A: Pearl
- B: Diamond
- C: Ruby
- D: Golden

49

Put these castles in order from north to south.

- A: Balmoral
- B: Windsor
- C: Caernarvon
- D: Warwick

50

Put these words in the order they first appear in the famous nursery rhyme.

- A: Sixpence
- B: Pocket
- C: Sing
- D: Rye

Turn to the answer section on page 269 to see if you've earned a place in the hot seat!

FASTEST FINGER FIRST

51

Put these sitcoms in the order they were first seen on television.

A: Blackadder
B: Dad's Army
C: Absolutely Fabulous
D: The Good Life

52

Put the reigns of these kings in chronological order.

A: Charles I
B: William the Conqueror
C: George VI
D: Henry V

53

Put these countries in the order they first won football's World Cup.

A: England
B: Brazil
C: France
D: Italy

54

Put these Dr Who actors in chronological order.

A: Jon Pertwee
B: Colin Baker
C: William Hartnell
D: Tom Baker

55

Starting with the earliest in the astrological year, put these zodiac signs in order.

A: Pisces
B: Aries
C: Leo
D: Capricorn

Turn to the answer section on page 269 to see if you've earned a place in the hot seat!

FASTEST FINGER FIRST

56

Starting with the earliest, put these newspapers in the order they were first published.

A: Daily Mail
B: The Sun
C: The Times
D: The Independent

57

Starting nearest the beginning, put these letters of the Greek alphabet in order.

A: Gamma
B: Omega
C: Beta
D: Theta

58

Put these 'Carry On' films in the order they were first released.

A: Carry On Columbus
B: Carry On Sergeant
C: Carry On Emmannuelle
D: Carry On Doctor

59

Put these words in alphabetical order.

A: Commodore
B: Commissar
C: Commander
D: Commissionaire

60

Starting with the lowest denomination, put these American coins in order.

A: Nickel
B: Dollar
C: Dime
D: Cent

Turn to the answer section on page 269 to see if you've earned a place in the hot seat!

FASTEST FINGER FIRST

61

Put these Oscar-winning films
in the order they were first released.

- A: My Fair Lady
- B: Casablanca
- C: The Sting
- D: Shakespeare in Love

62

Put these children's programmes
in the order they were first seen on TV.

- A: Stingray
- B: Grange Hill
- C: Blue Peter
- D: Crackerjack

63

Starting with the earliest, put these
medical celebrities in birthdate order.

- A: Florence Nightingale
- B: Christiaan Barnard
- C: Hippocrates
- D: Alexander Fleming

64

Starting with the smallest, put these amounts in order.

- A: Score
- B: Gross
- C: Baker's dozen
- D: Brace

65

Put these racing drivers in the order
they first became world champion.

- A: James Hunt
- B: Graham Hill
- C: Nigel Mansell
- D: Mika Hakkinen

Turn to the answer section on page 269 to see if you've earned a place in the hot seat!

FASTEST FINGER FIRST

66

Put these shipping forecast areas
in order from north to south.

- A: Humber
- B: Dover
- C: South-East Iceland
- D: Forth

67

Put these celebrities in the
order they presented 'Crackerjack'.

- A: Leslie Crowther
- B: Ed Stewart
- C: Eamonn Andrews
- D: Michael Aspel

68

Put these wars in chronological order.

- A: English Civil War
- B: Gulf War
- C: Napoleonic Wars
- D: Wars of the Roses

69

Put these plays in the order they were first performed.

- A: An Ideal Husband
- B: The Mousetrap
- C: Macbeth
- D: Pygmalion

70

Put these letters in the order they appear from
left to right on a standard computer keyboard.

- A: B
- B: V
- C: Z
- D: M

Turn to the answer section on page 269 to see if you've earned a place in the hot seat!

FASTEST FINGER FIRST

71

Starting with the earliest, put these actors in the order they were born.

A: Jack Lemmon

B: James Cagney

C: Harrison Ford

D: Tom Cruise

72

Put these historical events in chronological order.

A: American Civil War

B: First World War

C: Gunpowder Plot

D: French Revolution

73

Put these stage musicals in the order they were first performed.

A: Hair

B: The Phantom of the Opera

C: Evita

D: Oklahoma!

74

Put these US states in order from west to east.

A: Arizona

B: New York

C: California

D: Oklahoma

75

Put these British prime ministers in chronological order.

A: John Major

B: William Gladstone

C: James Callaghan

D: Ramsay MacDonald

Turn to the answer section on page 269 to see if you've earned a place in the hot seat!

FASTEST FINGER FIRST

76

Put these Beatles singles in
the order they were first released.

- A: Hey Jude
- B: Ticket to Ride
- C: Back in the USSR
- D: Love Me Do

77

Starting with the earliest, put these
fashion designers in the order they were born.

- A: Jasper Conran
- B: Christian Dior
- C: Coco Chanel
- D: Mary Quant

78

Starting with the earliest, put these
writers in the order they were born.

- A: Oscar Wilde
- B: Charles Dickens
- C: Seamus Heaney
- D: Henry Fielding

79

Put these lines of latitude in order from south to north.

- A: Tropic of Cancer
- B: Equator
- C: Tropic of Capricorn
- D: Arctic Circle

80

Starting with the earliest, put these
composers in the order they were born.

- A: George Frederick Handel
- B: Andrew Lloyd Webber
- C: Oscar Hammerstein II
- D: Ludwig van Beethoven

Turn to the answer section on page 269 to see if you've earned a place in the hot seat!

FASTEST FINGER FIRST

81

Starting with the earliest, put these foods in the order they are traditionally eaten during the year.

- A: Pumpkin
- B: Pancake
- C: Hot cross bun
- D: Christmas cake

82

Starting with the earliest, put these actresses in the order they were born.

- A: Joan Crawford
- B: Catherine Zeta Jones
- C: Judi Dench
- D: Edith Evans

83

Starting with the earliest, put these Wimbledon singles champions in the order they first won the title.

- A: Jana Novotna
- B: Maureen Connolly
- C: Billie Jean King
- D: Martina Navratilova

84

Starting with the closest, put these cities in order of their distance from London.

- A: Bangkok
- B: Baghdad
- C: Berlin
- D: Brisbane

85

Starting with the earliest, put these poets in the order they were born.

- A: Dylan Thomas
- B: Geoffrey Chaucer
- C: Lord Byron
- D: Homer

Turn to the answer section on page 269 to see if you've earned a place in the hot seat!

86

Starting with the earliest in the year, put the following in order.

- A: Good Friday
- B: Valentine's Day
- C: Bonfire Night
- D: Christmas Day

87

Starting with the lowest, put these four darts scores in numerical order.

- A: Treble six
- B: Double top
- C: Bull's-eye
- D: Double seven

88

Starting with the smallest, put these oceans in order by area.

- A: Atlantic
- B: Indian
- C: Pacific
- D: Arctic

89

Starting with the smallest, put these four distances in order.

- A: Metre
- B: Yard
- C: Mile
- D: Furlong

90

Put these film musicals in the order they were first released.

- A: Mary Poppins
- B: Fame
- C: Easter Parade
- D: The Wizard of Oz

Turn to the answer section on page 269 to see if you've earned a place in the hot seat!

FASTEST FINGER FIRST

91

Starting with the shortest,
put these monarchs' reigns in order.

A: Anne
B: Elizabeth I
C: Victoria
D: Richard III

92

Put these celebrities in the
order they presented 'Blue Peter'.

A: Sarah Greene
B: John Leslie
C: Valerie Singleton
D: Simon Groom

93

Put these British cities in order from west to east.

A: Oxford
B: Norwich
C: Bristol
D: Swansea

94

Put these Disney films in the
order they were first released.

A: The Jungle Book
B: The Lion King
C: Fantasia
D: Lady and the Tramp

95

Starting with the lowest,
put these Roman numerals in order.

A: C
B: IX
C: XV
D: M

Turn to the answer section on page 269 to see if you've earned a place in the hot seat!

FASTEST FINGER FIRST

96

Starting with the earliest, put these Eurovision Song Contest winners in order.

A: Brotherhood of Man
B: Dana
C: Sandie Shaw
D: Celine Dion

97

Put these days of the week in alphabetical order.

A: Tuesday
B: Sunday
C: Saturday
D: Thursday

98

Put these Bond films in the order they were first released.

A: A View to a Kill
B: The World Is Not Enough
C: Thunderball
D: Live and Let Die

99

Put these English counties in order from north to south.

A: Hampshire
B: Warwickshire
C: Durham
D: Derbyshire

100

Put these words in order to form the title of a Simon and Garfunkel hit.

A: Over
B: Water
C: Bridge
D: Troubled

Turn to the answer section on page 269 to see if you've earned a place in the hot seat!

15	£1 MILLION
14	£500,000
13	£250,000
12	£125,000
11	£64,000
10	**£32,000**
9	£16,000
8	£8,000
7	£4,000
6	£2,000
5	**£1,000**
4	£500
3	£300
2	£200
1 ◆	**£100**

1

Which of these is a mountain peak in Scotland?

A: Bill

B: Ben

C: Bob

D: Brian

2

Complete the name of this famous ice skating partnership: Torvill and ...?

A: Bishop

B: Vicar

C: Dean

D: Parson

3

Which of these garments shares its name with an earl and a Welsh town?

A: Sweater

B: Pullover

C: Jumper

D: Cardigan

4

Which of these is the name of a pop group?

A: Swinging Pebbles

B: Dancing Boulders

C: Rolling Stones

D: Spinning Rocks

5

Which of these is a famous London park?

A: Darby Park

B: Joan Park

C: Jekyll Park

D: Hyde Park

If you would like to use your 50:50 please turn to page 241
If you would like to Ask The Audience please turn to page 255
Turn to the answer section on page 269 to find out if you've won £100!

6

Who cleans out soot from chimneys?

A: Sooty

B: Sweep

C: Soo

D: Butch

7

Which of these is the name of a popular meat dish?

A: House pie

B: Cottage pie

C: Bungalow pie

D: Villa pie

8

'Mug' is a slang word for which part of the body?

A: Foot

B: Face

C: Finger

D: Funny bone

9

What do caterpillars grow up to be?

A: Butterflies

B: Frogs

C: Rabbits

D: Monkeys

10

What do Olympic long jumpers land on?

A: Sand

B: Feathers

C: Water

D: Jelly

If you would like to use your 50:50 please turn to page 241
If you would like to Ask The Audience please turn to page 255
Turn to the answer section on page 269 to find out if you've won £100!

11

What is the name of the pageboy in the pantomime 'Cinderella'?

- A: Zipper
- B: Toggles
- C: Popper
- D: Buttons

12

What can you metaphorically 'talk off' a donkey?

- A: Top forelock
- B: Hind leg
- C: Fore-quarter
- D: Hard shoulder

13

Which of these is a dance?

- A: Chicken waltz
- B: Turkey trot
- C: Hen hop
- D: Goose gallop

14

In the saying, what is the one thing left behind when you've packed everything else?

- A: Wallpaper
- B: Four-poster bed
- C: Kitchen sink
- D: Mother-in-law

15

Which member of the family gives his name to a longcase clock?

- A: Grandfather
- B: Uncle
- C: Nephew
- D: Papa

If you would like to use your 50:50 please turn to page 241
If you would like to Ask The Audience please turn to page 255
Turn to the answer section on page 269 to find out if you've won £100!

16

What mode of transport is traditionally used by fairy tale witches?

A: Penny-farthing

B: Scooter

C: Broomstick

D: Unicycle

17

Originating in cricket, what do you call three successive sporting points or victories?

A: Hat-trick

B: Cap-trick

C: Tammy-trick

D: Titfer-tat-trick

18

Which special piece of kit does a paratrooper have strapped to his back?

A: Hamper

B: Beer barrel

C: Parachute

D: Horse

19

Which animals do you associate with the Pied Piper of Hamelin?

A: Bats

B: Rats

C: Cats

D: Gnats

20

What was built across northern England to keep out invading Scots?

A: Caesar's Dyke

B: Nero's Canal

C: Caligula's Fence

D: Hadrian's Wall

If you would like to use your 50:50 please turn to page 241
If you would like to Ask The Audience please turn to page 255
Turn to the answer section on page 269 to find out if you've won £100!

1 ◆ £100

21

What does a display of 'five o'clock shadow' warrant?

A: Shave

B: Haircut

C: Sunbathe

D: Scrub down

22

What is the Eskimo word for house?

A: Kayak

B: Parka

C: Anorak

D: Igloo

23

According to the proverb, 'Every dog has...' what?

A: Bad breath

B: Fleas

C: His day

D: A cold wet nose

24

What was the name for a group of men, often on horseback, called on by the US sheriff to hunt down criminals?

A: Posse

B: Posset

C: Posser

D: Possum

25

Which golf club is used on the green to sink the ball into the hole?

A: Pitter

B: Patter

C: Potter

D: Putter

If you would like to use your 50:50 please turn to page 241
If you would like to Ask The Audience please turn to page 255
Turn to the answer section on page 269 to find out if you've won £100!

1 ♦ £100

26

What is the specific name for a large, and often international, gathering of Scouts?

- A: Buckaroo
- B: Jamboree
- C: Didgeridoo
- D: Dib-dib-dib-a-dee

27

What kind of eagle is the national bird of the USA?

- A: One-legged
- B: Hairy
- C: Bald
- D: Red-nosed

28

What is the name of the famous bell in the clock tower at the Houses of Parliament?

- A: Big Time
- B: Big Bang
- C: Big Ben
- D: Big Noise

29

Which letter usually denotes the basement in a British lift?

- A: B
- B: C
- C: G
- D: M

30

In mythology, everything that King Midas touched turned to what?

- A: Peanuts
- B: Beer
- C: Gold
- D: Blancmange

If you would like to use your 50:50 please turn to page 241
If you would like to Ask The Audience please turn to page 255
Turn to the answer section on page 269 to find out if you've won £100!

31

Which of these farm animals is not represented in the twelve signs of the zodiac?

A: Ostrich

B: Goat

C: Ram

D: Bull

32

Which of these boys' names is also a herb?

A: Bertram

B: Basil

C: Boris

D: Bartholomew

33

What was Rembrandt's famous occupation?

A: Painter

B: Electrician

C: Plumber

D: Window cleaner

34

Which football club shares its name with Bill Clinton's daughter?

A: Arsenal

B: Chelsea

C: Queen of the South

D: Watford

35

What was the surname of the nurse whose first name was Florence?

A: Ostrich

B: Woodpecker

C: Nightingale

D: Turkey

If you would like to use your 50:50 please turn to page 241
If you would like to Ask The Audience please turn to page 255
Turn to the answer section on page 269 to find out if you've won £100!

36

Which of these is not one of the Seven Deadly Sins?

A: Lust

B: Gluttony

C: Pride

D: Tax evasion

37

Complete this phrase: 'As drunk as a ...'?

A: Pop star

B: Lord

C: Footballer

D: Priest

38

Which snack food was named after the Earl who invented it?

A: Sausage roll

B: Sandwich

C: Pizza

D: Crisp

39

Which of these names is the personification of England?

A: John Major

B: John Bull

C: John Travolta

D: Elton John

40

Which of these is not a chesspiece?

A: King

B: Queen

C: Bishop

D: Actress

If you would like to use your 50:50 please turn to page 241
If you would like to Ask The Audience please turn to page 255
Turn to the answer section on page 269 to find out if you've won £100!

1 ◆ £100

41

Which of these is a famous French landmark?

A: Sears Tower

B: Eiffel Tower

C: Tower of London

D: Blackpool Tower

42

Who starred with Oliver Hardy in a series of comedy films?

A: Stan Tree

B: Stan Laurel

C: Stan Hedge

D: Stan Bush

43

Which bird is the national emblem of New Zealand?

A: Kiwi

B: Chicken

C: Turkey

D: Partridge

44

What should you do with maracas?

A: Eat them

B: Shake them

C: Sit on them

D: Wear them

45

What destroyed the ancient city of Pompeii?

A: Volcano

B: Football hooligans

C: Bulldozer

D: Pavarotti

If you would like to use your 50:50 please turn to page 241
If you would like to Ask The Audience please turn to page 255
Turn to the answer section on page 269 to find out if you've won £100!

46

Which birds are associated with the Tower of London?

A: Ravens

B: Budgerigars

C: Flamingos

D: Emus

47

In the song 'The Twelve Days of Christmas', seven what are a-swimming?

A: Dolphins

B: Swans

C: Penguins

D: Squid

48

Which bird's name is used for a type of pedestrian crossing in Britain?

A: Robin

B: Magpie

C: Pelican

D: Albatross

49

Which type of clothing is associated with the word 'Panama'?

A: Trousers

B: Vest

C: Hat

D: Anorak

50

Which flower shares its name with part of the eye?

A: Hollyhock

B: Iris

C: Fuchsia

D: Lupin

If you would like to use your 50:50 please turn to page 241
If you would like to Ask The Audience please turn to page 255
Turn to the answer section on page 269 to find out if you've won £100!

1 ◆ £100

51

Which form of transport is used
in the Isle of Man TT Races?

- A: Motorcycle
- B: Roller skates
- C: Hovercraft
- D: Tractor

52

In which city is there a famous Leaning Tower?

- A: Portsmouth
- B: Pisa
- C: Pasadena
- D: Peterborough

53

Who first co-presented
'The Big Breakfast' with Chris Evans?

- A: Gaby Roslin
- B: Thora Hird
- C: Joan Bakewell
- D: Judith Chalmers

54

What is the insect name for the small
Volkswagen, first produced in the 1930s?

- A: Earwig
- B: Beetle
- C: Termite
- D: Cockroach

55

Which of these was a leader of the
Sioux at the Battle of the Little Bighorn?

- A: Sitting Up
- B: Sitting Bull
- C: Sitting Duck
- D: Sitting Pretty

If you would like to use your 50:50 please turn to page 241
If you would like to Ask The Audience please turn to page 255
Turn to the answer section on page 269 to find out if you've won £100!

56

Who is Scarlett O'Hara's love in 'Gone With the Wind'?

A: Rooster Cogburn

B: Rocky Balboa

C: Rhett Butler

D: Roger Rabbit

57

What was the profession of Fabergé, famous for his eggs?

A: Farmer

B: Jeweller

C: Bird breeder

D: Chocolate manufacturer

58

The zebra belongs to which family of animals?

A: Giraffe

B: Elephant

C: Horse

D: Seal

59

The London store Hamleys is best known for selling what?

A: Toys

B: Bathroom fittings

C: Underwear

D: Fish and chips

60

Which dance was named after a city in South Carolina?

A: Jitterbug

B: Charleston

C: Lambeth walk

D: Highland fling

If you would like to use your 50:50 please turn to page 241
If you would like to Ask The Audience please turn to page 255
Turn to the answer section on page 269 to find out if you've won £100!

1 ◆ £100

61

Who played the leading role in the 'Superman' movies?

- A: Christopher Reeve
- B: Christopher Plummer
- C: Christopher Timothy
- D: Christopher Biggins

62

What is the name of the scientific study of sound and sound waves?

- A: Gymnastics
- B: Acoustics
- C: Fiddlesticks
- D: Drumsticks

63

Which of these animals has a type called 'hammerhead'?

- A: Rabbit
- B: Shark
- C: Bison
- D: Tiger

64

What is the name of the area around a city which is not meant to be built on?

- A: Green belt
- B: Blue sock
- C: White tie
- D: Red hat

65

Which sport shares its name with an insect?

- A: Rugby
- B: Cricket
- C: Tennis
- D: Lacrosse

If you would like to use your 50:50 please turn to page 241
If you would like to Ask The Audience please turn to page 255
Turn to the answer section on page 269 to find out if you've won £100!

66

What would you usually do with an aubergine?

A: Throw it

B: Play it

C: Eat it

D: Wear it

67

What is a hundredth of a metre called?

A: Centimetre

B: Gram

C: Litre

D: Inch

68

A general is a high ranking officer in which of the services?

A: Police

B: Army

C: Royal Navy

D: Royal Air Force

69

Prince Philip is the Duke of where?

A: Edinburgh

B: Cardiff

C: London

D: Belfast

70

Which of these is the name of a Christmas holiday?

A: Bowling Day

B: Cycling Day

C: Boxing Day

D: Curling Day

If you would like to use your 50:50 please turn to page 241
If you would like to Ask The Audience please turn to page 255
Turn to the answer section on page 269 to find out if you've won £100!

71

Which of these is a group of Spanish islands?

A: Canaries
B: Parrots
C: Budgies
D: Turkeys

72

Andrew Lloyd Webber composed 'Joseph and the Amazing Technicolor...' what?

A: Wagon
B: Dreamcoat
C: Grease
D: Salad

73

Which athletics event shares its name with a famous battle?

A: Steeplechase
B: Javelin
C: Marathon
D: Hurdles

74

John Cleese starred in the Oscar-winning film 'A Fish Called...' what?

A: Brenda
B: Wanda
C: Sandra
D: Amanda

75

What does the first letter B stand for in the abbreviation BBC?

A: Bovine
B: British
C: Broken
D: Binary

If you would like to use your 50:50 please turn to page 241
If you would like to Ask The Audience please turn to page 255
Turn to the answer section on page 269 to find out if you've won £100!

76

Which word means a hutlike shelter for a dog?

A: Hutch
B: Basket
C: Kennel
D: Coop

77

Which day of the week is Pancake Day?

A: Monday
B: Tuesday
C: Wednesday
D: Thursday

78

In Greek mythology, who was God of the Underworld?

A: Pluto
B: Goofy
C: Mickey
D: Donald

79

What kind of animal is Anna Sewell's 'Black Beauty'?

A: Sheep
B: Rabbit
C: Horse
D: Gerbil

80

Melbourne is a state capital in which country?

A: South Africa
B: USA
C: Mexico
D: Australia

If you would like to use your 50:50 please turn to page 241
If you would like to Ask The Audience please turn to page 255
Turn to the answer section on page 269 to find out if you've won £100!

1 ◆ £100

81

In the Bible, Daniel was thrown
into a den of which creatures?

A: Pigs

B: Goats

C: Lions

D: Bats

82

Which creature represents the zodiac sign Cancer?

A: Crab

B: Serpent

C: Tiger

D: Monkey

83

What is the name of San Francisco's famous bridge?

A: Platinum Passage

B: Golden Gate

C: Silver Span

D: Bronze Barrier

84

Who married Fred Flintstone?

A: Wilma

B: Barney

C: Pebbles

D: Dino

85

Which of these characters
featured in the TV series 'Stingray'?

A: Troy Tempest

B: Clive Cloud

C: Pete Puddle

D: Roger Rainbow

If you would like to use your 50:50 please turn to page 241
If you would like to Ask The Audience please turn to page 255
Turn to the answer section on page 269 to find out if you've won £100!

86

What is the unit of currency in Switzerland?

A: Luc

B: Franc

C: Marc

D: Jacques

87

What nationality was the monk Rasputin?

A: Russian

B: Irish

C: Australian

D: Mexican

88

How many witches are there in the opening scene of Shakespeare's 'Macbeth'?

A: Three

B: Five

C: Seven

D: Nine

If you would like to use your 50:50 please turn to page 241
If you would like to Ask The Audience please turn to page 255
Turn to the answer section on page 269 to find out if you've won £100!

15	£1 MILLION
14	£500,000
13	£250,000
12	£125,000
11	£64,000
10	**£32,000**
9	£16,000
8	£8,000
7	£4,000
6	£2,000
5	**£1,000**
4	£500
3	£300
2 ◆	**£200**
1 ◆	£100

1

Alitalia is the national airline of which country?

A: Italy
B: Sweden
C: Portugal
D: France

2

Which of these words can mean 'a large feather'?

A: Quibble
B: Quiff
C: Quill
D: Quince

3

Apple sauce traditionally accompanies which meat?

A: Turkey
B: Beef
C: Pork
D: Chicken

4

What is the eighth month of the year?

A: August
B: September
C: October
D: November

5

Which silent film star had the first name Charlie?

A: Fairbanks
B: Keaton
C: Chaplin
D: Valentino

If you would like to use your 50:50 please turn to page 242
If you would like to Ask The Audience please turn to page 256
Turn to the answer section on page 270 to find out if you've won £200!

6

What is a piña colada?

A: Tree
B: Parrot
C: Nut
D: Drink

7

Who would be most likely to use an aqualung?

A: Diver
B: Farmer
C: Doctor
D: Pilot

8

Which of these is a football club?

A: Liverpool Monday
B: Nottingham Tuesday
C: Sheffield Wednesday
D: Manchester Thursday

9

Which computer problem was much heralded in 1999?

A: Y2K maggot
B: Two-MM worm
C: Millennium bug
D: Countdown tic

10

Which of these is a process which might result in a president's removal from office?

A: Impearment
B: Impeachment
C: Implumment
D: Imprunement

If you would like to use your 50:50 please turn to page 242
If you would like to Ask The Audience please turn to page 256
Turn to the answer section on page 270 to find out if you've won £200!

11

What is the popular name for the wild cards in a standard pack of playing cards?

A: Knaves
B: Jesters
C: Jokers
D: Hoaxers

12

What is the North American name for the game of draughts?

A: Chockers
B: Chukkas
C: Checkers
D: Cheggers

13

Which word do you associate with towns that establish cultural links with similar towns in other countries?

A: Twin
B: Triplet
C: Quin
D: Sextuplet

14

The word 'canine' refers to which animal?

A: Cat
B: Rat
C: Hog
D: Dog

15

In the popular poem, which bird marries the Pussy-Cat?

A: Crow
B: Duck
C: Owl
D: Goose

If you would like to use your 50:50 please turn to page 242
If you would like to Ask The Audience please turn to page 256
Turn to the answer section on page 270 to find out if you've won £200!

2 ◆ £200

16

In which month do people traditionally dance around a pole in Britain?

A: April
B: May
C: June
D: July

17

Mint sauce traditionally accompanies which meat?

A: Goose
B: Venison
C: Lamb
D: Duck

18

Which football club plays home games at Old Trafford?

A: Newcastle United
B: Sheffield United
C: Manchester United
D: Leeds United

19

Which country has a basic unit of currency called the 'mark'?

A: France
B: Netherlands
C: Germany
D: Italy

20

Which Spice Girl has a son called Brooklyn?

A: Sporty
B: Posh
C: Scary
D: Baby

If you would like to use your 50:50 please turn to page 242
If you would like to Ask The Audience please turn to page 256
Turn to the answer section on page 270 to find out if you've won £200!

21

Which vegetable do you traditionally associate with Wales?

A: Carrot
B: Leek
C: Cauliflower
D: Swede

22

With which sport do you associate Ian Botham?

A: Rugby league
B: Tennis
C: Cricket
D: Golf

23

The abbreviation 'BC' signifies a date before the birth of whom?

A: Adam
B: Abraham
C: Jesus Christ
D: Moses

24

Which colour do you associate with being sad and melancholy?

A: Blue
B: Purple
C: Green
D: Yellow

25

Tinkerbell is a fairy in which children's story?

A: Sleeping Beauty
B: Peter Pan
C: Cinderella
D: Aladdin

If you would like to use your 50:50 please turn to page 242
If you would like to Ask The Audience please turn to page 256
Turn to the answer section on page 270 to find out if you've won £200!

26

Minestrone is a traditional Italian type of which food?

- A: Pastry
- B: Soup
- C: Fish
- D: Pudding

27

In the traditional tale, what is the name of Punch's wife?

- A: Julie
- B: Jackie
- C: Judy
- D: Jenny

28

The Prince of Wales is which member of the British royal family?

- A: William
- B: Edward
- C: Charles
- D: Andrew

29

Which clockwork fruit appears in the title of an Anthony Burgess novel?

- A: Orange
- B: Pineapple
- C: Plum
- D: Banana

30

Which of these is an opera by Puccini?

- A: Madame Ladybird
- B: Madame Beetle
- C: Madame Butterfly
- D: Madame Caterpillar

If you would like to use your 50:50 please turn to page 242
If you would like to Ask The Audience please turn to page 256
Turn to the answer section on page 270 to find out if you've won £200!

31

Which Beatle married Yoko Ono in 1969?

- A: George Harrison
- B: Ringo Starr
- C: Paul McCartney
- D: John Lennon

32

Which famous battle was fought in 1815?

- A: King's Cross
- B: Waterloo
- C: Victoria
- D: Euston

33

Which tune was used as the theme to the film 'Bridge on the River Kwai'?

- A: Colonel Mustard
- B: Colonel Blimp
- C: Colonel Bogey
- D: Colonel Sanders

34

According to the nursery rhyme, which city did Doctor Foster visit in a shower of rain?

- A: Wigan
- B: Gloucester
- C: Huddersfield
- D: Grimsby

35

Who is the companion of Sherlock Holmes?

- A: Dr Johnson
- B: Dr Watson
- C: Dr Foster
- D: Dr Marten

If you would like to use your 50:50 please turn to page 242
If you would like to Ask The Audience please turn to page 256
Turn to the answer section on page 270 to find out if you've won £200!

36

What was President Nixon's first name?

A: Jimmy

B: George

C: Ronald

D: Richard

37

Which sign of the zodiac is represented by a lion?

A: Leo

B: Virgo

C: Taurus

D: Aquarius

38

**Who was the native rescued
from cannibals by Robinson Crusoe?**

A: Man Sunday

B: Man Monday

C: Man Thursday

D: Man Friday

39

**Which word represents the
letter T in the phonetic alphabet?**

A: Turnip

B: Tortoise

C: Tango

D: Tomato

40

Granny Smith is a variety of which fruit?

A: Pear

B: Apple

C: Grape

D: Banana

If you would like to use your 50:50 please turn to page 242
If you would like to Ask The Audience please turn to page 256
Turn to the answer section on page 270 to find out if you've won £200!

41

What is the first letter of the Greek alphabet?

A: Alpha
B: Beta
C: Delta
D: Omega

42

How many years are there in three-quarters of a century?

A: 50
B: 65
C: 75
D: 80

43

What was the name of King Arthur's legendary sword?

A: Exodus
B: Excalibur
C: Exchequer
D: Executor

44

Who wrote books about Noddy?

A: Dick Francis
B: Enid Blyton
C: Agatha Christie
D: Jeffrey Archer

45

Which of these was once a member of the pop group Genesis?

A: Pauline Collins
B: Michael Collins
C: Joan Collins
D: Phil Collins

If you would like to use your 50:50 please turn to page 242
If you would like to Ask The Audience please turn to page 256
Turn to the answer section on page 270 to find out if you've won £200!

46

With which sport is Mike Tyson associated?

- A: Swimming
- B: Cricket
- C: Boxing
- D: Gymnastics

47

Which of these men was involved with the Gunpowder Plot?

- A: Guy Mitchell
- B: Guy Fawkes
- C: Guy Mannering
- D: Guy Standing

48

In which town was Shakespeare born?

- A: Henley-on-Thames
- B: Stratford-on-Avon
- C: Stockton-on-Tees
- D: Frinton-on-Sea

49

What is the capital of Spain?

- A: Monrovia
- B: Munich
- C: Madrid
- D: Malmö

50

In Greek mythology, who led the Argonauts?

- A: Jason
- B: Joseph
- C: Jonathan
- D: Jacob

If you would like to use your 50:50 please turn to page 242
If you would like to Ask The Audience please turn to page 256
Turn to the answer section on page 270 to find out if you've won £200!

51

Which South American country shares its name with a nut?

- A: Chile
- B: Brazil
- C: Ecuador
- D: Peru

52

Which of these was a ship commanded by Captain Bligh?

- A: HMS Galaxy
- B: HMS Bounty
- C: HMS Mars
- D: HMS Milky Way

53

In which month is St Valentine's Day?

- A: January
- B: February
- C: March
- D: April

54

Which musical instrument does Sherlock Holmes famously play?

- A: Bagpipes
- B: Drums
- C: Kazoo
- D: Violin

55

Which continent is home to the Zulu people?

- A: Asia
- B: Australia
- C: North America
- D: Africa

If you would like to use your 50:50 please turn to page 242
If you would like to Ask The Audience please turn to page 256
Turn to the answer section on page 270 to find out if you've won £200!

56

What is the Scottish name for New Year's Eve?

A: Hoots Mon   B: Up Hellya

C: Hootenanny   D: Hogmanay

57

What type of tree is known as a 'gum tree' in Australia?

A: Maple   B: Eucalyptus

C: Redwood   D: Elm

58

A raisin is a dried version of which fruit?

A: Grape   B: Plum

C: Cherry   D: Apricot

59

Flora was the Roman goddess of what?

A: Fashion   B: Fun

C: Flowers   D: Flirting

60

As what are Gary Rhodes and Jamie Oliver best known?

A: Bishops   B: Chefs

C: Newsreaders   D: Ballet dancers

If you would like to use your 50:50 please turn to page 242
If you would like to Ask The Audience please turn to page 256
Turn to the answer section on page 270 to find out if you've won £200!

61

Which branch of medicine is concerned with the treatment of children?

- A: Radiology
- B: Geriatrics
- C: Paediatrics
- D: Cardiology

62

Which Sussex town gives its name to a famous eleventh century battle?

- A: Worthing
- B: Hove
- C: Hastings
- D: Eastbourne

63

Hallowe'en is celebrated on the last day of which month?

- A: April
- B: June
- C: August
- D: October

64

Gorgonzola is a cheese from which country?

- A: Italy
- B: France
- C: Holland
- D: Greece

65

What is the world's largest living bird?

- A: Golden eagle
- B: Turkey
- C: Ostrich
- D: Albatross

If you would like to use your 50:50 please turn to page 242
If you would like to Ask The Audience please turn to page 256
Turn to the answer section on page 270 to find out if you've won £200!

66

Which surname connects film
actresses Bette, Geena and Judy?

A: Davis

B: Ford

C: Huston

D: Russell

67

Which of these months has thirty-one days?

A: April

B: June

C: September

D: December

68

In Roman numerals, which letter
represents the number five?

A: V

B: X

C: M

D: L

69

What is the name of the tree trunk
tossed in the Scottish sport?

A: Lumber

B: Haggis

C: Logwood

D: Caber

70

Which character is the heroine
of the film 'The Wizard of Oz'?

A: Sally

B: Dorothy

C: Hazel

D: Marion

If you would like to use your 50:50 please turn to page 242
If you would like to Ask The Audience please turn to page 256
Turn to the answer section on page 270 to find out if you've won £200!

71

In Sydney, what type of attraction is Bondi?

A: Opera house

B: Harbour bridge

C: Beach resort

D: Waterfall

72

What type of fruit is a honeydew?

A: Strawberry

B: Plum

C: Peach

D: Melon

73

Which of these is an Edinburgh landmark?

A: Pauline's Cardigan

B: Arthur's Seat

C: Michelle's Jeans

D: Mark's Fruit

74

Which of these is a film featuring John Hurt?

A: The Elephant Man

B: The Rhinoceros Man

C: The Hippopotamus Man

D: The Gorilla Man

75

Where on the body are slingbacks worn?

A: Knees

B: Shoulders

C: Feet

D: Hands

If you would like to use your 50:50 please turn to page 242
If you would like to Ask The Audience please turn to page 256
Turn to the answer section on page 270 to find out if you've won £200!

76

All Fool's Day is the first of which month?

A: January

B: February

C: March

D: April

77

In which country is paella a traditional dish?

A: France

B: Russia

C: Spain

D: Germany

78

What was the name of Del Boy's brother in the TV sitcom 'Only Fools and Horses'?

A: Rupert

B: Rodney

C: Robin

D: Roderick

79

Babylon was the site of which of the Seven Wonders of the World?

A: Hanging Gardens

B: Colossus

C: Mausoleum

D: Pharos

80

Which of the following is an island group in the Pacific?

A: Waiter Islands

B: Baker Islands

C: Cook Islands

D: Chef Islands

If you would like to use your 50:50 please turn to page 242
If you would like to Ask The Audience please turn to page 256
Turn to the answer section on page 270 to find out if you've won £200!

81

What is the nationality of Agatha Christie's detective Poirot?

A: American

B: Russian

C: German

D: Belgian

82

Pelé played for which international football team?

A: Brazil

B: Germany

C: Italy

D: England

83

What was the name of Francis Drake's famous ship?

A: Golden Calf

B: Golden Hind

C: Golden Mare

D: Golden Goose

84

In the Bible, where is Jesus born?

A: Nazareth

B: Nineveh

C: Bethlehem

D: Jerusalem

If you would like to use your 50:50 please turn to page 242
If you would like to Ask The Audience please turn to page 256
Turn to the answer section on page 270 to find out if you've won £200!

50:50		
15	£1 MILLION	
14	£500,000	
13	£250,000	
12	£125,000	
11	£64,000	
10	£32,000	
9	£16,000	
8	£8,000	
7	£4,000	
6	£2,000	
5	£1,000	
4	£500	
3 ◆	£300	
2 ◆	£200	
1 ◆	£100	

1

Which of these is an equestrian sport?

A: Basketball

B: Shinty

C: Cricket

D: Dressage

2

Who would traditionally sing a shanty?

A: Tinker

B: Tailor

C: Soldier

D: Sailor

3

What is a vinaigrette?

A: Honey jar

B: Alcoholic drink

C: Salad dressing

D: Meat plate

4

What is a female fox called?

A: Hart

B: Vixen

C: Mare

D: Jill

5

The River Clyde flows through which Scottish city?

A: Aberdeen

B: Edinburgh

C: Dundee

D: Glasgow

If you would like to use your 50:50 please turn to page 243
If you would like to Ask The Audience please turn to page 257
Turn to the answer section on page 270 to find out if you've won £300!

6

Which word refers to a racehorse that has never won a race?

A: Wife

B: Spinster

C: Bride

D: Maiden

7

Which part of Achilles was vulnerable?

A: Heart

B: Head

C: Heel

D: Hand

8

What is the surname of Richard of 'Richard and Judy' fame?

A: Whiteley

B: Langley

C: Madeley

D: Kingsley

9

Who was Nelson's flag captain on HMS Victory at Trafalgar?

A: Dickens

B: Thackeray

C: Austen

D: Hardy

10

Rory Bremner is best known as what?

A: Magician

B: Impressionist

C: Hypnotist

D: Contortionist

If you would like to use your 50:50 please turn to page 243
If you would like to Ask The Audience please turn to page 257
Turn to the answer section on page 270 to find out if you've won £300!

11

What was the name of Queen Victoria's husband?

A: Henry

B: George

C: Albert

D: Edward

12

What is a red admiral?

A: Fish

B: Bird

C: Butterfly

D: Drunken sailor

13

The word 'cardiac' means of or relating to which organ of the body?

A: Brain

B: Lung

C: Heart

D: Skin

14

What was the water-filled trench that provided fortification round a castle?

A: Keep

B: Transom

C: Moat

D: Portcullis

15

What would you do with 'gruel'?

A: Eat it

B: Wear it

C: Plant it

D: Hang wallpaper with it

If you would like to use your 50:50 please turn to page 243
If you would like to Ask The Audience please turn to page 257
Turn to the answer section on page 270 to find out if you've won £300!

16

What is the name of Margaret Thatcher's husband?

A: Boris

B: Denis

C: Francis

D: Douglas

17

Bavaria is a region of which country?

A: Norway

B: Turkey

C: Spain

D: Germany

18

The organisation RoSPA is the Royal Society for the Prevention of what?

A: Amnesia

B: Assassination

C: Accidents

D: Art

19

What is the correct way of calling 'Forty-all' in tennis?

A: Advantage

B: Deuce

C: Fore

D: Snap

20

In which building did the Coronation of Elizabeth II take place in 1953?

A: Tower of London

B: Westminster Abbey

C: Madame Tussaud's

D: Ritz Hotel

If you would like to use your 50:50 please turn to page 243
If you would like to Ask The Audience please turn to page 257
Turn to the answer section on page 270 to find out if you've won £300!

21

What is measured in decibels?

A: Height

B: Temperature

C: Sound

D: Wind speed

22

Which of these is a famous bridge in Venice?

A: Bridge of Moans

B: Bridge of Groans

C: Bridge of Whines

D: Bridge of Sighs

23

Which of these birds is flightless?

A: Emu

B: Nightingale

C: Sparrow

D: Lark

24

Who lives in Lambeth Palace?

A: The Queen

B: Mr and Mrs Beckham

C: Tony Blair

D: Archbishop of Canterbury

25

Which of these is a Hampshire tourist attraction?

A: Old Forest

B: New Forest

C: Black Forest

D: White Forest

If you would like to use your 50:50 please turn to page 243
If you would like to Ask The Audience please turn to page 257
Turn to the answer section on page 270 to find out if you've won £300!

26

The All Blacks are the rugby
union team of which country?

A: South Africa
B: Argentina
C: New Zealand
D: France

27

Which singer starred in the film 'Evita'?

A: Cher
B: Barbra Streisand
C: Celine Dion
D: Madonna

28

Which day follows Maundy Thursday?

A: Good Friday
B: Ash Friday
C: Advent Friday
D: Pancake Friday

29

Which of these models was married to Richard Gere?

A: Marie Helvin
B: Twiggy
C: Jerry Hall
D: Cindy Crawford

30

The canal which links the Caribbean to
the Pacific goes through which country?

A: Mexico
B: Honduras
C: Panama
D: Colombia

If you would like to use your 50:50 please turn to page 243
If you would like to Ask The Audience please turn to page 257
Turn to the answer section on page 270 to find out if you've won £300!

31

Which of these tourist attractions is in Staffordshire?

A: Alton Towers

B: Westminster Abbey

C: Stonehenge

D: Millennium Dome

32

What was the first name of the Spanish artist Dali?

A: Jose

B: Pedro

C: Iago

D: Salvador

33

Syd and Eddie are the first names of which comedy duo?

A: Smith and Jones

B: Reeves and Mortimer

C: Hale and Pace

D: Little and Large

34

According to the Bible, which part of his body was the source of Samson's strength?

A: Hair

B: Feet

C: Teeth

D: Ears

35

John Boy and Jim-Bob were members of which TV family?

A: Addams

B: Waltons

C: Munsters

D: Groves

If you would like to use your 50:50 please turn to page 243
If you would like to Ask The Audience please turn to page 257
Turn to the answer section on page 270 to find out if you've won £300!

36

Venison is the meat of which animal?

A: Sheep
B: Deer
C: Wild boar
D: Cow

37

Which of these people might use a hod?

A: Fisherman
B: Builder
C: Gardener
D: Baker

38

Which of the following is a type of sugar?

A: Detroit
B: Delaware
C: Denver
D: Demerara

39

Who played 007 in only one James Bond film?

A: Sean Connery
B: Roger Moore
C: George Lazenby
D: Timothy Dalton

40

Cuba is about one hundred miles away from which US state?

A: Alaska
B: California
C: Florida
D: Montana

If you would like to use your 50:50 please turn to page 243
If you would like to Ask The Audience please turn to page 257
Turn to the answer section on page 270 to find out if you've won £300!

41

Which word means of or relating to the eye or vision?

A: Oral

B: Nasal

C: Aural

D: Optical

42

In which country was the Sikh religion founded?

A: China

B: Russia

C: Japan

D: India

43

Debbie Rowe married which musical superstar?

A: Elvis Presley

B: Cliff Richard

C: Michael Jackson

D: Elton John

44

Who was the frequent film partner of Ginger Rogers?

A: Spencer Tracy

B: Mickey Rooney

C: Fred Astaire

D: Stan Laurel

45

Who is the first woman in the Bible?

A: Mary

B: Eve

C: Martha

D: Ruth

If you would like to use your 50:50 please turn to page 243
If you would like to Ask The Audience please turn to page 257
Turn to the answer section on page 270 to find out if you've won £300!

46

Which planet shares its name with a metallic element?

- A: Pluto
- B: Mercury
- C: Jupiter
- D: Saturn

47

What is the profession of Paul McCartney's daughter Stella?

- A: Dog handler
- B: Gardener
- C: Fashion designer
- D: Musician

48

Which of these French towns or cities is not on the coast?

- A: Calais
- B: Boulogne
- C: Paris
- D: Nice

49

In which country is the novel 'The Thorn Birds' chiefly set?

- A: Greece
- B: Singapore
- C: Australia
- D: Mongolia

50

In computing, what word is used for a set of binary digits, usually eight in number?

- A: Nybble
- B: Sipp
- C: Byte
- D: Mouthfull

If you would like to use your 50:50 please turn to page 243
If you would like to Ask The Audience please turn to page 257
Turn to the answer section on page 270 to find out if you've won £300!

51

Which of these utensils would be used to serve 'mulligatawny', 'borscht' or 'gazpacho'?

A: Sieve
B: Cleaver
C: Ladle
D: Tongs

52

What was the title of the heir to the French throne?

A: Delphine
B: Dauphin
C: Endorphin
D: Dolphin

53

Which popular TV soap is set in Weatherfield?

A: Home and Away
B: Brookside
C: Emmerdale
D: Coronation Street

54

Which of these names represents a letter of the phonetic alphabet?

A: Clement
B: Christie
C: Charlie
D: Clinton

55

Which of these foods was the title of a successful TV sitcom?

A: Cake
B: Muffin
C: Bread
D: Crumpet

If you would like to use your 50:50 please turn to page 243
If you would like to Ask The Audience please turn to page 257
Turn to the answer section on page 270 to find out if you've won £300!

56

Which famous mountain dominates
Cape Town in South Africa?

A: Table Mountain

B: Bed Mountain

C: Wardrobe Mountain

D: Chair Mountain

57

Which sign of the zodiac is represented by two fish?

A: Aquarius

B: Pisces

C: Gemini

D: Libra

58

Yorkshire, Manchester and Airedale
are all breeds of which dog?

A: Spaniel

B: Setter

C: Sheepdog

D: Terrier

59

Which of these is a book of the Bible?

A: Proverbs

B: Catchphrases

C: Sayings

D: Quotations

60

A chiropodist is concerned with which parts of the body?

A: Knees

B: Teeth

C: Feet

D: Cheeks

If you would like to use your 50:50 please turn to page 243
If you would like to Ask The Audience please turn to page 257
Turn to the answer section on page 270 to find out if you've won £300!

61

What is the relation of your father's brother's child to you?

A: Uncle

B: Half-brother

C: Second cousin

D: First cousin

62

What is a halibut?

A: Fish

B: Beetle

C: Goat

D: Cat

63

In terms of area, what is the largest country in the world?

A: Austria

B: France

C: Russia

D: Panama

64

Samuel Pepys is famous for writing what kind of book?

A: Thesaurus

B: Dictionary

C: Encyclopaedia

D: Diary

65

What is the name of the river that flows past Edinburgh?

A: First

B: Third

C: Forth

D: Fifth

If you would like to use your 50:50 please turn to page 243
If you would like to Ask The Audience please turn to page 257
Turn to the answer section on page 270 to find out if you've won £300!

66

What was the nationality of the artist Pablo Picasso?

A: Italian
B: French
C: Spanish
D: German

67

Who starred as William Wallace in the Oscar-winning film 'Braveheart'?

A: Michael Douglas
B: Arnold Schwarzenegger
C: Bruce Willis
D: Mel Gibson

68

Which composer's first two names were Wolfgang Amadeus?

A: Beethoven
B: Tchaikovsky
C: Mozart
D: Handel

69

In the United States, what type of establishment is a penitentiary?

A: Telephone exchange
B: Bank
C: Prison
D: Museum

70

Who would be most likely to wear a matinée coat?

A: Fishmonger
B: Baby
C: Matron
D: Frogman

If you would like to use your 50:50 please turn to page 243
If you would like to Ask The Audience please turn to page 257
Turn to the answer section on page 270 to find out if you've won £300!

71

Which of these is not a type of hat?

A: Bowler

B: Batter

C: Boater

D: Beret

72

A cygnet is the young of which bird?

A: Goose

B: Duck

C: Turkey

D: Swan

73

Which of these places was created by C.S. Lewis?

A: Wonderland

B: Toyland

C: Gotham City

D: Narnia

74

Which literary character has a pet called a pushmi-pullyu?

A: Dr Who

B: Dr Finlay

C: Dr Dolittle

D: Dr Jekyll

75

What is the chemical formula for water?

A: HCL

B: H_2O_2

C: H_2O

D: H_2SO_4

If you would like to use your 50:50 please turn to page 243
If you would like to Ask The Audience please turn to page 257
Turn to the answer section on page 270 to find out if you've won £300!

76

Which fruit is dried to make a prune?

A: Apricot
B: Cherry
C: Plum
D: Banana

77

What is helium?

A: Metal
B: Gas
C: Plant
D: Gemstone

78

In mythology, Medusa's hair was made from what?

A: Snakes
B: Straw
C: Scales
D: Seaweed

79

How many sides are there on a heptagon?

A: One
B: Three
C: Five
D: Seven

80

Which river flows through Dublin?

A: Liffey
B: Thames
C: Severn
D: Trent

If you would like to use your 50:50 please turn to page 243
If you would like to Ask The Audience please turn to page 257
Turn to the answer section on page 270 to find out if you've won £300!

50:50		

15	£1 MILLION
14	£500,000
13	£250,000
12	£125,000
11	£64,000
10	£32,000
9	£16,000
8	£8,000
7	£4,000
6	£2,000
5	£1,000
4 ◆	£500
3 ◆	£300
2 ◆	£200
1 ◆	£100

4 ◆ £500

1

A haiku is a verse form from which country?

A: New Zealand
B: Honduras
C: Iceland
D: Japan

2

What did Christopher Cockerell invent?

A: Jet engine
B: Helicopter
C: Hovercraft
D: Nylon

3

Charles Schulz was most famous for drawing which cartoon strip?

A: Andy Capp
B: Garfield
C: Peanuts
D: Fred Basset

4

Which of these words describes a person who can speak many languages?

A: Polyester
B: Polyglot
C: Polynesia
D: Polygon

5

What title is given to the longest continuously serving member of the House of Commons?

A: Father of the House
B: Bench Elder
C: Senior Commoner
D: Old Father Time

If you would like to use your 50:50 please turn to page 244
If you would like to Ask The Audience please turn to page 258
Turn to the answer section on page 271 to find out if you've won £500!

6

According to the song, what does Molly Malone wheel through 'Dublin's fair city'?

- A: Pushchair
- B: Supermarket trolley
- C: Wheelbarrow
- D: Zimmer frame

7

Which game was Francis Drake famously playing on Plymouth Hoe in 1588?

- A: Cricket
- B: Golf
- C: Bowls
- D: Croquet

8

The rat, rooster and dragon are signs in which calendar?

- A: Islamic
- B: Jewish
- C: Chinese
- D: Hindu

9

Which two initials denote the 'casualty' department of a hospital?

- A: P & O
- B: V & A
- C: R & B
- D: A & E

10

Motorway signs have white lettering on which colour background?

- A: Green
- B: Red
- C: Blue
- D: Yellow

If you would like to use your 50:50 please turn to page 244
If you would like to Ask The Audience please turn to page 258
Turn to the answer section on page 271 to find out if you've won £500!

11

What was the Duchess of York's maiden name?

A: Donaldson
B: Ferguson
C: Jamieson
D: Robertson

12

What type of tree does an acorn grow into?

A: Chestnut
B: Beech
C: Elm
D: Oak

13

What was the name of the cow in 'The Magic Roundabout'?

A: Ermintrude
B: Modestine
C: Esmerelda
D: Gertrude

14

What do you associate with the Klondike, the Yukon and the Californian 49-ers?

A: Oil
B: Diamonds
C: Gold
D: Silver

15

What do American cheerleaders usually hold in each hand for their routines at sports events?

A: Loudhailers
B: Model flags
C: Pompoms
D: Drumsticks

If you would like to use your 50:50 please turn to page 244
If you would like to Ask The Audience please turn to page 258
Turn to the answer section on page 271 to find out if you've won £500!

16

With which sport do you associate Nick Faldo?

A: Golf

B: Table tennis

C: Swimming

D: Squash

17

Complete the title of the Quentin Tarantino film: 'Reservoir ...'?

A: Frogs

B: Horses

C: Moles

D: Dogs

18

Which part of the body is used as a command for a dog to walk close by its owner?

A: Foot

B: Toe

C: Heel

D: Ankle

19

What sort of pastries do you associate with the Queen of Hearts?

A: Pasties

B: Croissants

C: Pies

D: Tarts

20

Which trophy is contested by the winners of the AFC and NFC in American Football?

A: Super Cup

B: Super Dish

C: Super Bowl

D: Super Plate

If you would like to use your 50:50 please turn to page 244
If you would like to Ask The Audience please turn to page 258
Turn to the answer section on page 271 to find out if you've won £500!

4 ◆ £500

21

Which spirit lived in Aladdin's lamp?

A: Genie
B: Pixie
C: Goblin
D: Troll

22

What specific type of people are the 'paparazzi'?

A: Pizza chefs
B: Fashion designers
C: Photographers
D: Gossip columnists

23

Which animals are renowned for building dams across streams?

A: Otters
B: Voles
C: Water rats
D: Beavers

24

What is proverbially put 'among the pigeons' to cause trouble?

A: Owl
B: Cat
C: Fox
D: Scarecrow

25

Where would you be likely to find an 'asterisk'?

A: Planted in a garden
B: Written on a page
C: Fitted in an engine
D: Hanging from the ceiling

If you would like to use your 50:50 please turn to page 244
If you would like to Ask The Audience please turn to page 258
Turn to the answer section on page 271 to find out if you've won £500!

4 ◆ £500

26

Which season of the year is associated with hibernation?

A: Spring

B: Summer

C: Autumn

D: Winter

27

Which planet is known as the Red Planet?

A: Mars

B: Jupiter

C: Uranus

D: Neptune

28

Which of these was not one of the famous Marx Brothers?

A: Groucho

B: Karl

C: Chico

D: Harpo

29

To what does the word 'nuptial' refer?

A: Birth

B: Childhood

C: Marriage

D: Old age

30

Which service is divided into constabularies?

A: Ambulance

B: Fire

C: Coastguard

D: Police

If you would like to use your 50:50 please turn to page 244
If you would like to Ask The Audience please turn to page 258
Turn to the answer section on page 271 to find out if you've won £500!

4 ◆ £500

31

Which of these is a famous opera by Bizet?

A: Boatmen

B: Carmen

C: Dustmen

D: Barmen

32

Santiago is the capital of which country?

A: Chile

B: Yemen

C: El Salvador

D: San Marino

33

What name is given to a person who gains access to computer files without permission?

A: Snooper

B: Hacker

C: Creeper

D: Sneaker

34

Which football team is nicknamed 'The Gunners'?

A: Arsenal

B: Liverpool

C: Chelsea

D: Manchester City

35

Which country comprises a North Island and a South Island?

A: Cyprus

B: Sri Lanka

C: New Zealand

D: Iceland

If you would like to use your 50:50 please turn to page 244
If you would like to Ask The Audience please turn to page 258
Turn to the answer section on page 271 to find out if you've won £500!

36

With which type of music was Tammy Wynette associated?

A: Opera

B: Country

C: Jazz

D: Folk

37

What was produced by the Bugatti company?

A: Cars

B: Pianos

C: Glassware

D: Wine

38

What kind of garment is a tuxedo?

A: Shoe

B: Hat

C: Jacket

D: Tie

39

In Greece, what is 'ouzo'?

A: Bread

B: Olive oil

C: Alcoholic drink

D: Aubergine

40

What was the name of the group Morrissey sang with before going solo?

A: The Cohens

B: The Smiths

C: The Patels

D: The Joneses

If you would like to use your 50:50 please turn to page 244
If you would like to Ask The Audience please turn to page 258
Turn to the answer section on page 271 to find out if you've won £500!

4 ◆ £500

41

Which British colony was returned to China in 1997?

A: Macao
B: Singapore
C: Hong Kong
D: Burma

42

Which organisation was founded by Lord Baden-Powell?

A: RAC
B: Oxfam
C: Boy Scouts
D: National Trust

43

Which Greek is said to have run down the street shouting 'Eureka'?

A: Plato
B: Aristotle
C: Euripides
D: Archimedes

44

The Indian town of Darjeeling gives its name to what?

A: Army helmet
B: Monkey
C: Fabric
D: Tea

45

For what would a wok normally be used?

A: Sailing
B: Fishing
C: Cooking
D: Sleeping

If you would like to use your 50:50 please turn to page 244
If you would like to Ask The Audience please turn to page 258
Turn to the answer section on page 271 to find out if you've won £500!

46

What is the surname of the captain of the Home Guard in 'Dad's Army'?

A: Wilson

B: Pike

C: Jones

D: Mainwaring

47

What is a 'cagoule'?

A: Raincoat

B: Boat

C: Cooking pot

D: Reptile

48

What was the name of the first Norman king of England?

A: Cedric

B: William

C: Rollo

D: Norman

49

The island of Cyprus is in which body of water?

A: Mediterranean Sea

B: Red Sea

C: Black Sea

D: Caspian Sea

50

Where on the body is a sou'wester worn?

A: Head

B: Foot

C: Hand

D: Shoulder

If you would like to use your 50:50 please turn to page 244
If you would like to Ask The Audience please turn to page 258
Turn to the answer section on page 271 to find out if you've won £500!

51

Which market town hosts a three-day rock festival every summer?

- A: Salisbury
- B: Glastonbury
- C: Tewkesbury
- D: Canterbury

52

In traditional folklore, who is the King of the Fairies?

- A: William Tell
- B: Robin Hood
- C: Oberon
- D: Punch

53

What type of instrument is a harpsichord?

- A: Keyboard
- B: Brass
- C: Woodwind
- D: Percussion

54

What does a cartographer make?

- A: Maps
- B: Stamps
- C: Playing cards
- D: Medals

55

With which of these drinks is Stilton cheese traditionally served?

- A: Port
- B: Vodka
- C: Champagne
- D: Gin

If you would like to use your 50:50 please turn to page 244
If you would like to Ask The Audience please turn to page 258
Turn to the answer section on page 271 to find out if you've won £500!

56

Stanley Gibbons is associated with the trade of which product?

A: Umbrellas
B: Stamps
C: Toys
D: Stationery

57

Congress is the name for the Upper and Lower Houses of which country?

A: Israel
B: Japan
C: Iceland
D: United States

58

In the TV soap 'Dallas', the former wife of which singer played Jenna?

A: Elvis Presley
B: Bill Haley
C: Roy Orbison
D: Buddy Holly

59

What is the name of the bear in the Disney animation 'The Jungle Book'?

A: Mowgli
B: Baloo
C: Shere Khan
D: Bagheera

60

What is the name of the famous geyser in Yellowstone National Park?

A: Old Testament
B: Old Faithful
C: Old Vic
D: Old Maid

If you would like to use your 50:50 please turn to page 244
If you would like to Ask The Audience please turn to page 258
Turn to the answer section on page 271 to find out if you've won £500!

61

'Beefsteak' is a large variety of which of these foods?

A: Lemon

B: Avocado

C: Marrow

D: Tomato

62

What type of creature is a barracuda?

A: Bird

B: Fish

C: Insect

D: Rodent

63

What was a blunderbuss?

A: Gun

B: Bird

C: Battering ram

D: Bicycle

64

**Which musical features the song
'You've Got To Pick a Pocket or Two'?**

A: Les Misérables

B: Annie

C: Oliver!

D: Miss Saigon

65

Which famous battle was fought in 1940?

A: Somme

B: Bosworth

C: Britain

D: Jutland

If you would like to use your 50:50 please turn to page 244
If you would like to Ask The Audience please turn to page 258
Turn to the answer section on page 271 to find out if you've won £500!

66

What is the bird nickname of Newcastle United football club?

A: Budgies

B: Magpies

C: Sparrows

D: Wrens

67

What does a philatelist collect?

A: Books

B: Coins

C: Stamps

D: Autographs

68

General Franco ruled which country?

A: Yugoslavia

B: Spain

C: Italy

D: Albania

69

What nationality was the artist Van Gogh?

A: Swiss

B: Dutch

C: Norwegian

D: French

70

Thomas Chippendale was best known for making what?

A: Clothes

B: Furniture

C: Jewellery

D: Porcelain

If you would like to use your 50:50 please turn to page 244
If you would like to Ask The Audience please turn to page 258
Turn to the answer section on page 271 to find out if you've won £500!

4 ◆ £500

71

In which country is risotto a traditional dish?

- A: Italy
- B: Poland
- C: France
- D: Greece

72

In which country did origami originate?

- A: Japan
- B: Italy
- C: Jamaica
- D: Egypt

73

The Falkland Islands are in which ocean?

- A: Arctic
- B: Indian
- C: Pacific
- D: Atlantic

74

What was the name of Basil Fawlty's wife in the TV sitcom 'Fawlty Towers'?

- A: Stella
- B: Stephanie
- C: Sylvia
- D: Sybil

75

How many years of marriage are celebrated by a pearl wedding anniversary?

- A: Twenty-five
- B: Thirty
- C: Fifty
- D: Sixty

If you would like to use your 50:50 please turn to page 244
If you would like to Ask The Audience please turn to page 258
Turn to the answer section on page 271 to find out if you've won £500!

76

What does the C stand for in the abbreviation CAB?

A: Company

B: Citizens

C: Central

D: Charter

If you would like to use your 50:50 please turn to page 244
If you would like to Ask The Audience please turn to page 258
Turn to the answer section on page 271 to find out if you've won £500!

15	£1 MILLION
14	£500,000
13	£250,000
12	£125,000
11	£64,000
10	**£32,000**
9	£16,000
8	£8,000
7	£4,000
6	£2,000
5 ◆	**£1,000**
4 ◆	£500
3 ◆	£300
2 ◆	£200
1 ◆	£100

5 ◆ £1,000

1

Which entertainer was famous for playing a ukulele?

A: Max Miller

B: George Formby

C: Jack Benny

D: Charlie Chester

2

Which TV drama series is set in Aidensfield?

A: Casualty

B: The Bill

C: Heartbeat

D: Byker Grove

3

In which part of the body would you find the tibia bone?

A: Shoulder

B: Arm

C: Leg

D: Head

4

In which sport might one use a 'spider'?

A: Squash

B: Hockey

C: Darts

D: Snooker

5

What name is given to a drink of cider and lager?

A: Fleabite

B: Mousebite

C: Snakebite

D: Horsebite

If you would like to use your 50:50 please turn to page 245
If you would like to Ask The Audience please turn to page 259
Turn to the answer section on page 271 to find out if you've won £1,000!

6

Which German city has the highest population?

- A: Berlin
- B: Düsseldorf
- C: Essen
- D: Rostock

7

The Greek god Pan is depicted with the legs of which creature?

- A: Badger
- B: Goat
- C: Frog
- D: Pig

8

Which of these islands lies on the equator?

- A: Borneo
- B: Corsica
- C: Iceland
- D: Tasmania

9

Which of these chemical elements is a gas?

- A: Barium
- B: Cobalt
- C: Neon
- D: Zinc

10

Who is third in line of succession to the throne?

- A: Prince Charles
- B: Prince William
- C: Prince Harry
- D: Prince Philip

If you would like to use your 50:50 please turn to page 245
If you would like to Ask The Audience please turn to page 259
Turn to the answer section on page 271 to find out if you've won £1,000!

11

Which part of a juniper bush is used to flavour gin?

A: Berry

B: Root

C: Leaf

D: Stalk

12

The humerus is a bone in which part of the body?

A: Arm

B: Foot

C: Back

D: Head

13

What is the name of the ex-King of Greece?

A: Aristotle

B: Constantine

C: Demis

D: Stavros

14

In which county is Keswick?

A: Durham

B: Lancashire

C: Cheshire

D: Cumbria

15

With which war is King Henry V associated?

A: Crusades

B: Boer War

C: 100 Years' War

D: Crimean War

If you would like to use your 50:50 please turn to page 245
If you would like to Ask The Audience please turn to page 259
Turn to the answer section on page 271 to find out if you've won £1,000!

16

What type of creature is a 'bunting'?

A: Fish
B: Bird
C: Insect
D: Reptile

17

Which of these explorers was the first to reach the Americas?

A: Columbus
B: Diaz
C: Vespucci
D: Magellan

18

In which city does Aston Villa Football Club have its home ground?

A: Sheffield
B: Manchester
C: Birmingham
D: London

19

What is the unit of thermal resistance commonly used to grade duvets and thermal clothing?

A: Tag
B: Tig
C: Tog
D: Tug

20

What is the underground home of a rabbit called?

A: Burrow
B: Drey
C: Sett
D: Lair

If you would like to use your 50:50 please turn to page 245
If you would like to Ask The Audience please turn to page 259
Turn to the answer section on page 271 to find out if you've won £1,000!

5 ◆ £1,000

21

'Papoose' is a North American Indian term for which of these?

A: Tent

B: Baby

C: Axe

D: Headdress

22

Which of these London Underground stations is south of the Thames?

A: Baker Street

B: Oxford Circus

C: Waterloo

D: Knightsbridge

23

Which animal grows a coat of ermine during the winter?

A: Otter

B: Squirrel

C: Beaver

D: Stoat

24

In which county is the resort of Skegness?

A: Devon

B: Lincolnshire

C: Kent

D: Suffolk

25

In the abbreviation 'G-force', what does the G stand for?

A: Gold

B: Gas

C: Group

D: Gravity

If you would like to use your 50:50 please turn to page 245
If you would like to Ask The Audience please turn to page 259
Turn to the answer section on page 271 to find out if you've won £1,000!

26

The bolero is a dance that originated in which country?

- A: Russia
- B: Spain
- C: France
- D: Hungary

27

CO_2 is the chemical formula for which gas?

- A: Hydrogen
- B: Ozone
- C: Nitrogen
- D: Carbon dioxide

28

What is a 'gavotte'?

- A: Necklace
- B: Dance
- C: Boat
- D: Waterproof shoe

29

What was the nationality of poet Dylan Thomas?

- A: Welsh
- B: Scottish
- C: Irish
- D: English

30

What is the specific name for a person who hides aboard a ship or aircraft to get free passage?

- A: Stowaway
- B: Castaway
- C: Runaway
- D: Faraway

If you would like to use your 50:50 please turn to page 245
If you would like to Ask The Audience please turn to page 259
Turn to the answer section on page 271 to find out if you've won £1,000!

5 ◆ £1,000

31

What is the specific name for a
baby badger, fox, lion or polar bear?

A: Puppy

B: Kitten

C: Cub

D: Fledgling

32

Havana is the capital of which country?

A: Haiti

B: Cuba

C: Mexico

D: Puerto Rico

33

In which North American city are
the headquarters of the United Nations?

A: Washington

B: Toronto

C: Chicago

D: New York

34

Which emblem was reinstated
on British eggs in January 2000?

A: Chicken

B: Bulldog

C: Crown

D: Lion

35

Arachnophobia is the fear of what?

A: Birds

B: Rats

C: Reptiles

D: Spiders

If you would like to use your 50:50 please turn to page 245
If you would like to Ask The Audience please turn to page 259
Turn to the answer section on page 271 to find out if you've won £1,000!

5 ◆ £1,000

36

On which continent is Sierra Leone?

A: Asia

B: South America

C: Africa

D: Europe

37

What is a single lens worn to correct defective vision in one eye?

A: Binoculars

B: Bifocals

C: Monocle

D: Lorgnette

38

What is the curved line that forms the boundary of a circle?

A: Radius

B: Circumference

C: Diameter

D: Tangent

39

Henry Morton Stanley was sent on an expedition to find which other explorer?

A: Christopher Columbus

B: Captain Oates

C: Walter Raleigh

D: Dr Livingstone

40

Who was the Greek god of love?

A: Apollo

B: Eros

C: Poseidon

D: Hades

If you would like to use your 50:50 please turn to page 245
If you would like to Ask The Audience please turn to page 259
Turn to the answer section on page 271 to find out if you've won £1,000!

41

Which of these musical terms means 'loud'?

A: Mezzo
B: Largo
C: Piano
D: Forte

42

What is the name of a reading desk in a church?

A: Cassock
B: Vestry
C: Lectern
D: Font

43

Which of these is the unit of currency in Israel?

A: Knesset
B: Shekel
C: Kibbutz
D: Jericho

44

What is a fandango?

A: Shoe
B: Snake
C: Dance
D: Plant

45

What is measured on the Beaufort Scale?

A: Wind
B: Earthquakes
C: Temperature
D: Pressure

If you would like to use your 50:50 please turn to page 245
If you would like to Ask The Audience please turn to page 259
Turn to the answer section on page 271 to find out if you've won £1,000!

46

What did Alexander Fleming discover?

A: Vitamins
B: Penicillin
C: Insulin
D: Blood groups

47

Cricket bats are traditionally made from which wood?

A: Ash
B: Oak
C: Maple
D: Willow

48

Charles Darwin was the botanist on which ship?

A: The Corgi
B: The Chihuahua
C: The Beagle
D: The Rottweiler

49

Which king abdicated in 1936?

A: Charles II
B: William IV
C: George V
D: Edward VIII

50

In which month do Americans celebrate Thanksgiving?

A: November
B: December
C: January
D: February

If you would like to use your 50:50 please turn to page 245
If you would like to Ask The Audience please turn to page 259
Turn to the answer section on page 271 to find out if you've won £1,000!

5 ◆ £1,000

51

Which word can precede 'guard' and 'keeping' to form two new words?

A: Life   B: Peace

C: Safe   D: Fire

52

Which planet is named after the Roman goddess of beauty and love?

A: Venus   B: Saturn

C: Uranus   D: Neptune

53

Where in the body is the cornea?

A: Eye   B: Mouth

C: Ear   D: Nose

54

What was the title of the last ruler of Iran?

A: Sultan   B: Emir

C: Sheikh   D: Shah

55

The Ghost of Christmas Past appears to which Dickens character?

A: Miss Havisham   B: Bill Sikes

C: Ebenezer Scrooge   D: Uriah Heep

If you would like to use your 50:50 please turn to page 245
If you would like to Ask The Audience please turn to page 259
Turn to the answer section on page 271 to find out if you've won £1,000!

56

In Greek mythology, what type of creature was Pegasus?

A: Dragon
B: Bull
C: Horse
D: Eagle

57

Which grain is normally used to make porridge?

A: Barley
B: Millet
C: Oats
D: Rice

58

In which field was Anna Pavlova famous?

A: Ballet
B: Science
C: Art
D: Opera

59

The Kalahari Desert is on which continent?

A: Africa
B: Asia
C: Europe
D: Australia

60

Who was told, 'Beware the Ides of March'?

A: Nero
B: Cleopatra
C: Julius Caesar
D: Juno

If you would like to use your 50:50 please turn to page 245
If you would like to Ask The Audience please turn to page 259
Turn to the answer section on page 271 to find out if you've won £1,000!

61

In which county is Falmouth?

A: Norfolk
B: Cornwall
C: Shropshire
D: West Yorkshire

62

Traditionally, who might wear a wimple?

A: Nun
B: Chef
C: Surgeon
D: Jockey

63

What was the name of the hill where Jesus was crucified?

A: Gethsemane
B: Calvary
C: Bethlehem
D: Nazareth

64

Which of these colours is represented in the five Olympic rings?

A: White
B: Purple
C: Green
D: Brown

65

Which of these is a salary or allowance paid to a clergyman?

A: Surplice
B: Diocese
C: Stipend
D: Curate

If you would like to use your 50:50 please turn to page 245
If you would like to Ask The Audience please turn to page 259
Turn to the answer section on page 271 to find out if you've won £1,000!

66

Which town in Ireland gives its name to a type of crystal glass?

- A: Cork
- B: Limerick
- C: Ballymena
- D: Waterford

67

Who wrote the novel 'The Mayor of Casterbridge'?

- A: D.H. Lawrence
- B: Thomas Hardy
- C: Kingsley Amis
- D: Emily Brontë

68

Which of these countries has the most sheep?

- A: Australia
- B: Malta
- C: Japan
- D: Panama

69

What would an Indian man do with his 'dhoti'?

- A: Eat it
- B: Ride it
- C: Drink it
- D: Wear it

70

Where in Britain is the famous 'Woolsack'?

- A: Yorkshire Dales
- B: House of Lords
- C: Leeds City Hall
- D: Westminster Abbey

If you would like to use your 50:50 please turn to page 245
If you would like to Ask The Audience please turn to page 259
Turn to the answer section on page 271 to find out if you've won £1,000!

5 ◆ £1,000

71

Which book follows Genesis in the Bible?

A: Numbers

B: Joshua

C: Exodus

D: Judges

72

The French port of Nantes lies on the estuary of which river?

A: Volga

B: Loire

C: Danube

D: Liffey

If you would like to use your 50:50 please turn to page 245
If you would like to Ask The Audience please turn to page 259
Turn to the answer section on page 271 to find out if you've won £1,000!

50:50		

15	£1 MILLION
14	£500,000
13	£250,000
12	£125,000
11	£64,000
10	**£32,000**
9	£16,000
8	£8,000
7	£4,000
6 ◆	**£2,000**
5 ◆	£1,000
4 ◆	£500
3 ◆	£300
2 ◆	£200
1 ◆	£100

1

In 1999, who did Lennox Lewis beat to become undisputed heavyweight champion of the world?

A: Evander Holyfield

B: Mike Tyson

C: Frank Bruno

D: Oliver McCall

2

According to the rhyme, on which day was Solomon Grundy married?

A: Monday

B: Tuesday

C: Wednesday

D: Thursday

3

What was the first name of Lady Astor, the first female MP to take her seat?

A: Nancy

B: Margot

C: Mary

D: Violet

4

Which garden feature is also the word used as a suffix to denote a scandal?

A: Shed

B: Fence

C: Gate

D: Patio

5

What is the shape of a British twenty pence piece?

A: Pentagon

B: Hexagon

C: Heptagon

D: Octagon

If you would like to use your 50:50 please turn to page 246
If you would like to Ask The Audience please turn to page 260
Turn to the answer section on page 271 to find out if you've won £2,000!

6

What is the traditional flavour of a sweet called a humbug?

A: Butterscotch

B: Liquorice

C: Mint

D: Aniseed

7

How do you express the fraction one-half as a decimal?

A: 0.125

B: 0.25

C: 0.5

D: 1.5

8

What is the real name of the comic book hero Batman?

A: Clark Kent

B: Dick Grayson

C: Bruce Wayne

D: Bob Kane

9

What would you be using if you required an STD code?

A: Telephone

B: Calculator

C: Bank cashpoint

D: Library

10

Where did acupuncture originate?

A: China

B: India

C: Thailand

D: Japan

If you would like to use your 50:50 please turn to page 246
If you would like to Ask The Audience please turn to page 260
Turn to the answer section on page 271 to find out if you've won £2,000!

11

In which city are the Inspector Morse books set?

A: Edinburgh   B: Oxford

C: Cambridge   D: Bath

12

What is former President Ford's first name?

A: George   B: Geoffrey

C: Jimmy   D: Gerald

13

Ray Reardon was a world champion in which sport?

A: Bowls   B: Chess

C: Snooker   D: Darts

14

Which group had a number one album called 'Parklife'?

A: Pulp   B: Portishead

C: Blur   D: Radiohead

15

The America's Cup is awarded in which sport?

A: Yachting   B: Baseball

C: Golf   D: Ice hockey

If you would like to use your 50:50 please turn to page 246
If you would like to Ask The Audience please turn to page 260
Turn to the answer section on page 271 to find out if you've won £2,000!

16

Which type of bag is named
after a British prime minister?

A: Gladstone

B: Palmerston

C: Melbourne

D: Disraeli

17

What is said to be the sincerest form of flattery?

A: Invention

B: Insight

C: Imitation

D: Investigation

18

What nationality was the
writer Hans Christian Andersen?

A: Danish

B: Finnish

C: Dutch

D: Swedish

19

What kind of musical instrument is a fife?

A: Drum

B: Flute

C: Piano

D: Harp

20

Which sport do the Harlem Globetrotters play?

A: Volleyball

B: Baseball

C: Basketball

D: Ice hockey

If you would like to use your 50:50 please turn to page 246
If you would like to Ask The Audience please turn to page 260
Turn to the answer section on page 271 to find out if you've won £2,000!

21

Which band was formed by Mark Knopfler?

A: Simply Red
B: Dire Straits
C: U2
D: Police

22

Where was Pope John Paul II born?

A: Belgium
B: Italy
C: Spain
D: Poland

23

Tamworth is a breed of which animal?

A: Sheep
B: Goat
C: Horse
D: Pig

24

Which city has the same name as a soccer match between two local teams?

A: Sheffield
B: York
C: Bristol
D: Derby

25

Catherine the Great was the empress of which country?

A: France
B: Russia
C: Austria
D: Germany

If you would like to use your 50:50 please turn to page 246
If you would like to Ask The Audience please turn to page 260
Turn to the answer section on page 271 to find out if you've won £2,000!

26

On which continent are the Andes mountains?

A: Africa

B: South America

C: Asia

D: Europe

27

Which of Disney's seven dwarfs wears glasses?

A: Grumpy

B: Bashful

C: Doc

D: Happy

28

Which of these is an informal expression for 'one thousand pounds'?

A: Pony

B: Ton

C: Grand

D: Monkey

29

In France, what is a 'gendarme'?

A: Postman

B: Mayor

C: Farmer

D: Policeman

30

Who wrote the novel 'Robinson Crusoe'?

A: Jonathan Swift

B: Henry Fielding

C: Daniel Defoe

D: Alexander Pope

If you would like to use your 50:50 please turn to page 246
If you would like to Ask The Audience please turn to page 260
Turn to the answer section on page 271 to find out if you've won £2,000!

31

What was the name of Alan Alda's character in TV's 'M*A*S*H'?

A: Eagleeye

B: Hawkeye

C: Fisheye

D: Brighteye

32

Goa is a state in which country?

A: India

B: Malaysia

C: Bangladesh

D: South Korea

33

What kind of creature is a Gloucester Old Spot?

A: Sheep

B: Horse

C: Goat

D: Pig

34

Isabel Péron was the president of which country?

A: Argentina

B: Cuba

C: Peru

D: Haiti

35

Key West is a part of which US state?

A: Georgia

B: Virginia

C: Florida

D: Rhode Island

If you would like to use your 50:50 please turn to page 246
If you would like to Ask The Audience please turn to page 260
Turn to the answer section on page 271 to find out if you've won £2,000!

36

Who was the star of the film 'Forrest Gump'?

A: Tom Hanks
B: Mel Gibson
C: Brad Pitt
D: Tom Cruise

37

What does the D stand for in the abbreviation DBE?

A: Dame
B: Doctor
C: Duchess
D: Duke

38

What flavour is the liqueur Tia Maria?

A: Orange
B: Aniseed
C: Vanilla
D: Coffee

39

Which pseudonym was adopted by the vet and author James Alfred Wight?

A: Hewitt
B: Hallett
C: Herriot
D: Hibbert

40

Who co-starred with Julia Roberts in the film 'Notting Hill'?

A: Hugh Grant
B: Kenneth Branagh
C: Liam Neeson
D: Anthony Hopkins

If you would like to use your 50:50 please turn to page 246
If you would like to Ask The Audience please turn to page 260
Turn to the answer section on page 271 to find out if you've won £2,000!

41

Which of these is the title of a hit single by Robbie Williams?

A: Fairies
B: Angels
C: Cowboys
D: Devils

42

What is the star sign of someone born on the fourth of July?

A: Leo
B: Aries
C: Virgo
D: Cancer

43

Who composed the orchestral suite 'The Planets'?

A: Ravel
B: Elgar
C: Bizet
D: Holst

44

With which sport is Jack Dempsey associated?

A: Baseball
B: Golf
C: Tennis
D: Boxing

45

Which musician's real name is Richard Starkey?

A: Rick Parfitt
B: Buddy Rich
C: Ringo Starr
D: Rick Wakeman

If you would like to use your 50:50 please turn to page 246
If you would like to Ask The Audience please turn to page 260
Turn to the answer section on page 271 to find out if you've won £2,000!

46

The wombat is native to which continent?

A: Africa

B: Asia

C: Australia

D: Europe

47

With which sport is Michael Jordan associated?

A: Basketball

B: Ice hockey

C: Baseball

D: Athletics

48

Who wrote the novel 'The Day of the Jackal'?

A: Frederick Forsyth

B: Jeffrey Archer

C: Dick Francis

D: Stephen King

49

Which metallic element has the chemical symbol Fe?

A: Aluminium

B: Gold

C: Mercury

D: Iron

50

Snowy and tawny are types of which bird?

A: Pigeon

B: Cuckoo

C: Swan

D: Owl

If you would like to use your 50:50 please turn to page 246
If you would like to Ask The Audience please turn to page 260
Turn to the answer section on page 271 to find out if you've won £2,000!

51

Who created the character Bertie Wooster?

A: Dorothy L. Sayers
B: Agatha Christie
C: P.G. Wodehouse
D: P.D. James

52

Who famously rode a horse called Black Bess?

A: Wyatt Earp
B: Napoleon
C: Dick Turpin
D: Wellington

53

What was the first name of the painter Constable?

A: Thomas
B: Frank
C: John
D: Peter

54

What was the first name of the composer Chopin?

A: Frederic
B: Franz
C: Johann
D: Ludwig

55

Which of these is a Major League Los Angeles baseball team?

A: Dodgers
B: Braves
C: Reds
D: Yankees

If you would like to use your 50:50 please turn to page 246
If you would like to Ask The Audience please turn to page 260
Turn to the answer section on page 271 to find out if you've won £2,000!

6 ◆ £2,000

56

The bassoon belongs to which section of an orchestra?

- A: String
- B: Percussion
- C: Brass
- D: Woodwind

57

Arthur C. Clarke is famous for writing which type of book?

- A: Espionage
- B: Science fiction
- C: Romance
- D: Horror

58

Pi r squared (πr^2) is the formula
for the surface area of what?

- A: Cube
- B: Circle
- C: Triangle
- D: Pyramid

59

From which London station would
you catch a train to Liverpool?

- A: Euston
- B: Vauxhall
- C: Blackfriars
- D: Victoria

60

Kelsey Grammer is the star of which US sitcom?

- A: Friends
- B: Home Improvement
- C: Frasier
- D: Due South

If you would like to use your 50:50 please turn to page 246
If you would like to Ask The Audience please turn to page 260
Turn to the answer section on page 271 to find out if you've won £2,000!

6 ♦ £2,000

61

Peter the Great ruled which country?

A: Russia
B: France
C: Austria
D: Italy

62

In astronomy, what is named after Edmund Halley?

A: Planet
B: Comet
C: Star
D: Moon

63

Who starred in the television sitcom 'Spin City'?

A: Brooke Shields
B: Tim Allen
C: Michael J. Fox
D: Jennifer Aniston

64

The Solent separates which island from England?

A: Isle of Wight
B: Anglesey
C: Iona
D: Lundy

65

Who created the character Bilbo Baggins?

A: Lewis Carroll
B: Enid Blyton
C: J.R.R. Tolkien
D: Roald Dahl

If you would like to use your 50:50 please turn to page 246
If you would like to Ask The Audience please turn to page 260
Turn to the answer section on page 271 to find out if you've won £2,000!

66

The Wightman Cup was awarded in which sport?

A: Tennis
B: Golf
C: Sailing
D: Cricket

67

What was the first name of the explorer Dr Livingstone?

A: James
B: David
C: Stanley
D: Robert

68

Where is Osborne House, Queen Victoria's former home?

A: Windsor
B: Norfolk
C: Scotland
D: Isle of Wight

If you would like to use your 50:50 please turn to page 246
If you would like to Ask The Audience please turn to page 260
Turn to the answer section on page 271 to find out if you've won £2,000!

50:50		
15	£1 MILLION	
14	£500,000	
13	£250,000	
12	£125,000	
11	£64,000	
10	**£32,000**	
9	£16,000	
8	£8,000	
7 ◆ £4,000		
6 ◆ £2,000		
5 ◆ £1,000		
4 ◆ £500		
3 ◆ £300		
2 ◆ £200		
1 ◆ £100		

1

Which animal is the emblem of the
Democratic Party in the United States?

A: Rattlesnake

B: Donkey

C: Armadillo

D: Kangaroo

2

Which imaginary line on the Earth's surface
lies largely at 180 degrees longitude?

A: Antarctic Circle

B: Tropic of Capricorn

C: 39th Parallel

D: International Date Line

3

Which people study the planets to assess their
influence on human characteristics and activities?

A: Astronomers

B: Horologists

C: Astrologers

D: Cosmologists

4

Iran was known by which name until 1935?

A: Persia

B: Siam

C: Abyssinia

D: Arabia

5

Which initials denote the government
agency that licenses drivers and vehicles?

A: GCHQ

B: RSVP

C: DVLA

D: OHMS

If you would like to use your 50:50 please turn to page 247
If you would like to Ask The Audience please turn to page 261
Turn to the answer section on page 272 to find out if you've won £4,000!

6

Which two Shakespearean characters are names in the phonetic alphabet?

- A: Antony and Cleopatra
- B: Romeo and Juliet
- C: Troilus and Cressida
- D: Oberon and Titania

7

What type of alcoholic drink is 'amontillado'?

- A: Brandy
- B: Port
- C: Vodka
- D: Sherry

8

Which number is dialled to ask for a telephone number in Britain?

- A: 100
- B: 0800
- C: 192
- D: 151

9

What is 25% of five dozen?

- A: 10
- B: 15
- C: 20
- D: 25

10

In which city do worshippers pray at the Wailing Wall?

- A: Cairo
- B: Jerusalem
- C: Damascus
- D: Baghdad

If you would like to use your 50:50 please turn to page 247
If you would like to Ask The Audience please turn to page 261
Turn to the answer section on page 272 to find out if you've won £4,000!

11

Which nut is used to make marzipan?

A: Walnut

B: Hazelnut

C: Brazil nut

D: Almond

12

Montreal is in which Canadian province?

A: Quebec

B: Nova Scotia

C: Alberta

D: New Brunswick

13

Nancy is a character in which Charles Dickens novel?

A: Oliver Twist

B: Barnaby Rudge

C: Hard Times

D: Bleak House

14

In the northern hemisphere, in which month is the vernal equinox?

A: March

B: June

C: September

D: December

15

What are hairstreaks and fritillaries?

A: Cocktails

B: Beetles

C: Butterflies

D: Apples

If you would like to use your 50:50 please turn to page 247
If you would like to Ask The Audience please turn to page 261
Turn to the answer section on page 272 to find out if you've won £4,000!

16

With which type of music was Fats Waller associated?

A: Country

B: Folk

C: Opera

D: Jazz

17

Which family featured in the TV series 'The Darling Buds of May'?

A: Bennet

B: Larkin

C: March

D: Brady

18

What type of creature is an eland?

A: Antelope

B: Monkey

C: Fish

D: Dog

19

As what was Arturo Toscanini famous?

A: Conductor

B: Aviator

C: Scientist

D: Philosopher

20

A samovar would be used to make what?

A: Furniture

B: Tea

C: Carpet

D: Shoes

If you would like to use your 50:50 please turn to page 247
If you would like to Ask The Audience please turn to page 261
Turn to the answer section on page 272 to find out if you've won £4,000!

21

Who wrote 'The Pilgrim's Progress'?

A: Geoffrey Chaucer

B: John Bunyan

C: William Shakespeare

D: Christopher Marlowe

22

What does the letter M stand for in the abbreviation GMT?

A: Maximum

B: Medium

C: Mean

D: Meridian

23

What was the first name of the designer Dior?

A: Yves

B: Christian

C: Hubert

D: Pierre

24

Yum-Yum is a character in which Gilbert and Sullivan operetta?

A: Patience

B: The Mikado

C: Ruddigore

D: Iolanthe

25

The aardvark is a mammal native to which continent?

A: Africa

B: South America

C: Asia

D: Australia

If you would like to use your 50:50 please turn to page 247
If you would like to Ask The Audience please turn to page 261
Turn to the answer section on page 272 to find out if you've won £4,000!

26

Drambuie is a liqueur based on which spirit?

- A: Rum
- B: Gin
- C: Vodka
- D: Whisky

27

Which adjective means 'resembling a wolf'?

- A: Ursine
- B: Equine
- C: Feline
- D: Lupine

28

Who was the last prime minister of the 1960s?

- A: Margaret Thatcher
- B: Harold Wilson
- C: Edward Heath
- D: Anthony Eden

29

Which of these writers is famous for nonsense verse?

- A: A.A. Milne
- B: Edward Lear
- C: Robert Bridges
- D: Kenneth Grahame

30

Which of these instruments is the longest?

- A: Flute
- B: Piccolo
- C: Bassoon
- D: Clarinet

If you would like to use your 50:50 please turn to page 247
If you would like to Ask The Audience please turn to page 261
Turn to the answer section on page 272 to find out if you've won £4,000!

7 ◆ £4,000

31

In which of these sports are
there seven players in a team?

A: Baseball

B: Cricket

C: Netball

D: Hockey

32

Which fictional hero was created by Captain W.E. Johns?

A: Tarzan

B: Invisible Man

C: Biggles

D: Superman

33

What name was given to the
girlfriend of an American gangster?

A: Moll

B: Hilary

C: Jill

D: Sally

34

In Irish folklore, the wailing of
which spirit warns of impending death?

A: Leprechaun

B: Banshee

C: Poltergeist

D: Sandman

35

The Elgin Marbles were brought
to Britain from which country?

A: Greece

B: India

C: Egypt

D: Italy

If you would like to use your 50:50 please turn to page 247
If you would like to Ask The Audience please turn to page 261
Turn to the answer section on page 272 to find out if you've won £4,000!

36

Which American president gave the Gettysburg Address?

- A: Washington
- B: Lincoln
- C: Taft
- D: Jefferson

37

What type of bird is an eider?

- A: Heron
- B: Swan
- C: Goose
- D: Duck

38

In which fictional town is the cartoon series 'The Simpsons' set?

- A: Bedrock
- B: Springfield
- C: Jellystone
- D: South Park

39

What is the capital of Canada?

- A: Toronto
- B: Vancouver
- C: Ottawa
- D: Winnipeg

40

Which of these writers was born first?

- A: Geoffrey Chaucer
- B: Jonathan Swift
- C: William Shakespeare
- D: John Milton

If you would like to use your 50:50 please turn to page 247
If you would like to Ask The Audience please turn to page 261
Turn to the answer section on page 272 to find out if you've won £4,000!

41

Who was the Roman god of war?

A: Cupid
B: Mars
C: Pluto
D: Apollo

42

Which language is the mother tongue of the gypsies?

A: Serbo-Croat
B: Breton
C: Gaelic
D: Romany

43

Which of these words means 'good news'?

A: Bible
B: Psalm
C: Testament
D: Gospel

44

An elver is the baby of which creature?

A: Mole
B: Hare
C: Otter
D: Eel

45

What shape is cannelloni pasta?

A: Butterfly
B: Ribbon
C: Tube
D: Shell

If you would like to use your 50:50 please turn to page 247
If you would like to Ask The Audience please turn to page 261
Turn to the answer section on page 272 to find out if you've won £4,000!

46

In the novel by D.H. Lawrence, what is the occupation of Lady Chatterley's lover?

A: Farmer
B: Gamekeeper
C: Miner
D: Sailor

47

Benazir Bhutto was the prime minister of which country?

A: Sri Lanka
B: Pakistan
C: Venezuela
D: Jamaica

48

Stanley is the capital of which British Crown Colony?

A: Gibraltar
B: Montserrat
C: Falkland Islands
D: Bermuda

49

What colour is the element sulphur?

A: Blue
B: White
C: Yellow
D: Red

50

In 1999, Prince Edward was created Earl of where?

A: York
B: Mercia
C: Wessex
D: Anglia

If you would like to use your 50:50 please turn to page 247
If you would like to Ask The Audience please turn to page 261
Turn to the answer section on page 272 to find out if you've won £4,000!

51

Who played the title role in the 1960s film musical 'Dr Dolittle'?

A: David Niven

B: Danny Kaye

C: Kenneth More

D: Rex Harrison

52

Which English coin was worth 21 shillings?

A: Tanner

B: Farthing

C: Florin

D: Guinea

53

Balliol is a college of which university?

A: Durham

B: London

C: Oxford

D: Cambridge

54

What was the name of Franklin D. Roosevelt's wife?

A: Jessica

B: Margaret

C: Winifred

D: Eleanor

55

Lady Godiva is said to have ridden naked through which town?

A: Leicester

B: Nottingham

C: Worcester

D: Coventry

If you would like to use your 50:50 please turn to page 247
If you would like to Ask The Audience please turn to page 261
Turn to the answer section on page 272 to find out if you've won £4,000!

56

Which of these literally means 'river horse'?

A: Elephant

B: Hippopotamus

C: Crocodile

D: Rhinoceros

57

What is the capital of Australia?

A: Sydney

B: Adelaide

C: Brisbane

D: Canberra

58

Who wrote the novel 'Pride and Prejudice'?

A: Jane Austen

B: Charles Dickens

C: George Eliot

D: Anthony Trollope

59

Where is the National Motor Museum?

A: Dagenham

B: Oxford

C: Warrington

D: Beaulieu

60

What name is given to a young hare?

A: Kitten

B: Bunny

C: Leveret

D: Pup

If you would like to use your 50:50 please turn to page 247
If you would like to Ask The Audience please turn to page 261
Turn to the answer section on page 272 to find out if you've won £4,000!

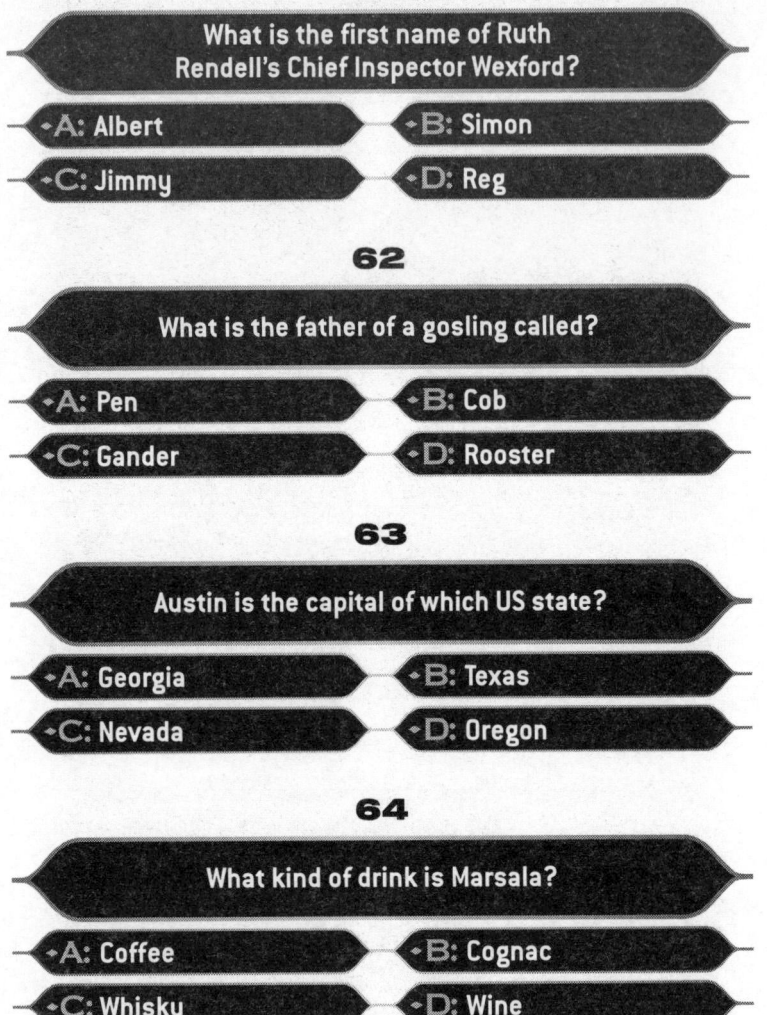

61

What is the first name of Ruth Rendell's Chief Inspector Wexford?

A: Albert

B: Simon

C: Jimmy

D: Reg

62

What is the father of a gosling called?

A: Pen

B: Cob

C: Gander

D: Rooster

63

Austin is the capital of which US state?

A: Georgia

B: Texas

C: Nevada

D: Oregon

64

What kind of drink is Marsala?

A: Coffee

B: Cognac

C: Whisky

D: Wine

If you would like to use your 50:50 please turn to page 247
If you would like to Ask The Audience please turn to page 261
Turn to the answer section on page 272 to find out if you've won £4,000!

50:50

15   £1 MILLION

14   £500,000

13   £250,000

12   £125,000

11   £64,000

10   **£32,000**

9   £16,000

8 ◆ £8,000

7 ◆ £4,000

6 ◆ £2,000

5 ◆ £1,000

4 ◆ £500

3 ◆ £300

2 ◆ £200

1 ◆ £100

8 ◆ £8,000

1

What was the name of the dog in the TV series 'Hart to Hart'?

A: Speedway
B: Highway
C: Freeway
D: Roadway

2

What kind of animal is a natterjack?

A: Hare
B: Snake
C: Ferret
D: Toad

3

Which of these countries does not use the franc as its basic unit of currency?

A: Switzerland
B: Liechtenstein
C: Belgium
D: Austria

4

In which battle were Drake's Revenge and Effingham's Ark Royal part of the victorious fleet?

A: Jutland
B: Spanish Armada
C: The Nile
D: Trafalgar

5

Which Latin word, meaning 'things to be done', is a list of topics to be covered at a meeting?

A: Menu
B: Etcetera
C: Index
D: Agenda

If you would like to use your 50:50 please turn to page 248
If you would like to Ask The Audience please turn to page 262
Turn to the answer section on page 272 to find out if you've won £8,000!

6

Which state occasion takes place annually on the Queen's official birthday?

- A: Opening of Parliament
- B: Remembrance Day
- C: Lord Mayor's Show
- D: Trooping the Colour

7

Which number do the letters MD represent in Roman numerals?

- A: 950
- B: 1,050
- C: 1,500
- D: 5,000

8

Which complex was opened in 1936 as the British film industry's equivalent of Hollywood?

- A: Pinewood
- B: Ivywood
- C: Oakwood
- D: Cedarwood

9

Basildon is in which English county?

- A: West Sussex
- B: East Sussex
- C: Essex
- D: Middlesex

10

Dave Brubeck is associated with which type of music?

- A: Soul
- B: Blues
- C: Opera
- D: Jazz

If you would like to use your 50:50 please turn to page 248
If you would like to Ask The Audience please turn to page 262
Turn to the answer section on page 272 to find out if you've won £8,000!

11

With which athletics event do you associate the Fosbury flop?

A: Pole vault

B: Marathon

C: High jump

D: Hurdles

12

To which royal house did Mary I belong?

A: York

B: Tudor

C: Lancaster

D: Plantagenet

13

Which tree features on the flag of Lebanon?

A: Poplar

B: Lilac

C: Cedar

D: Pine

14

What kind of insect is a scarab?

A: Beetle

B: Moth

C: Fly

D: Grasshopper

15

What is the meaning of the musical term 'allegro'?

A: Slowly

B: Quietly

C: Loudly

D: Quickly

If you would like to use your 50:50 please turn to page 248
If you would like to Ask The Audience please turn to page 262
Turn to the answer section on page 272 to find out if you've won £8,000!

16

What is the state capital of Arizona?

- A: Las Vegas
- B: Reno
- C: Little Rock
- D: Phoenix

17

What was the first name of the composer Grieg?

- A: Niels
- B: Olaf
- C: Edvard
- D: Erik

18

Quicksilver is another name for which element?

- A: Sodium
- B: Platinum
- C: Mercury
- D: Krypton

19

Who wrote the novel 'Gulliver's Travels'?

- A: Lewis Carroll
- B: Samuel Richardson
- C: Jonathan Swift
- D: Henry Fielding

20

With which country did Britain collaborate to build Concorde?

- A: Germany
- B: France
- C: Italy
- D: Sweden

If you would like to use your 50:50 please turn to page 248
If you would like to Ask The Audience please turn to page 262
Turn to the answer section on page 272 to find out if you've won £8,000!

21

Which country's international car registration is 'E'?

A: Egypt

B: Spain

C: Ecuador

D: Israel

22

In which city is the Hallé Orchestra based?

A: Birmingham

B: Edinburgh

C: Liverpool

D: Manchester

23

The DDR and the GDR united to form which country?

A: Vietnam

B: Yemen

C: Germany

D: Czechoslovakia

24

Which Saturday morning show
was presented by Chris Tarrant?

A: Saturday Banana

B: Swap Shop

C: Tiswas

D: Why Don't You...?

25

What is Australia's national airline?

A: KLM

B: Sabena

C: Qantas

D: Lufthansa

If you would like to use your 50:50 please turn to page 248
If you would like to Ask The Audience please turn to page 262
Turn to the answer section on page 272 to find out if you've won £8,000!

26

In which country is Urdu the official language?

A: Kenya

B: South Africa

C: Pakistan

D: Nepal

27

In which city is the football team Hibernian based?

A: Edinburgh

B: Glasgow

C: Aberdeen

D: Dundee

28

Who wrote the novel 'Lord of the Flies'?

A: Anthony Burgess

B: William Golding

C: Graham Greene

D: George Orwell

29

Which country was the centre of the Ottoman Empire?

A: Iran

B: China

C: Morocco

D: Turkey

30

Cliff Thorburn was a world champion in which sport?

A: Table tennis

B: Darts

C: Snooker

D: Squash

If you would like to use your 50:50 please turn to page 248
If you would like to Ask The Audience please turn to page 262
Turn to the answer section on page 272 to find out if you've won £8,000!

31

The word 'hepatic' refers to which organ of the body?

A: Heart
B: Liver
C: Kidney
D: Brain

32

In mythology, which creatures were depicted as birds with women's faces?

A: Fates
B: Harpies
C: Graces
D: Gorgons

33

Palermo is the capital of which Mediterranean island?

A: Sicily
B: Corsica
C: Crete
D: Sardinia

34

Which is the last book of the Bible?

A: Acts
B: Corinthians
C: Revelation
D: Romans

35

Which system is used as the digital base in computers?

A: Decimal
B: Denary
C: Octal
D: Binary

If you would like to use your 50:50 please turn to page 248
If you would like to Ask The Audience please turn to page 262
Turn to the answer section on page 272 to find out if you've won £8,000!

36

Edgar Rice Burroughs created which famous character?

- A: Biggles
- B: Tarzan
- C: Superman
- D: Billy Bunter

37

What is the capital of Tasmania?

- A: Dunedin
- B: Brisbane
- C: Auckland
- D: Hobart

38

In which country is Shakespeare's play 'Hamlet' set?

- A: France
- B: Denmark
- C: Austria
- D: Italy

39

What nationality was the composer Schubert?

- A: French
- B: Austrian
- C: Norwegian
- D: Italian

40

Which of these stately homes is in Derbyshire?

- A: Woburn
- B: Chatsworth
- C: Knebworth
- D: Blenheim

If you would like to use your 50:50 please turn to page 248
If you would like to Ask The Audience please turn to page 262
Turn to the answer section on page 272 to find out if you've won £8,000!

41

Cork is a natural product of which tree?

A: Beech
B: Maple
C: Chestnut
D: Oak

42

Which breed of cat has varieties called seal point and blue point?

A: Siamese
B: Manx
C: Chinchilla
D: Burmese

43

Whose UK hit singles include 'Vincent' and 'American Pie'?

A: David Essex
B: Donny Osmond
C: Dave Edmunds
D: Don McLean

44

The Java Trench is the deepest part of which ocean?

A: Indian
B: Arctic
C: Atlantic
D: Pacific

45

Who wrote the novel 'The Grapes of Wrath'?

A: F. Scott Fitzgerald
B: Ernest Hemingway
C: John Steinbeck
D: William Faulkner

If you would like to use your 50:50 please turn to page 248
If you would like to Ask The Audience please turn to page 262
Turn to the answer section on page 272 to find out if you've won £8,000!

46

William IV belonged to which royal house?

A: York

B: Hanover

C: Windsor

D: Tudor

47

Which 'Python' went from 'Pole to Pole' in a TV series?

A: Michael Palin

B: Eric Idle

C: John Cleese

D: Terry Jones

48

Where did the Mau Mau rebellion take place?

A: India

B: New Zealand

C: Mexico

D: Kenya

49

What nationality was the composer Liszt?

A: Italian

B: Spanish

C: Finnish

D: Hungarian

50

Who directed the film 'Gandhi'?

A: Tim Burton

B: Bryan Forbes

C: Richard Attenborough

D: Stephen Spielberg

If you would like to use your 50:50 please turn to page 248
If you would like to Ask The Audience please turn to page 262
Turn to the answer section on page 272 to find out if you've won £8,000!

51

Which football team plays home matches at Goodison Park?

A: Everton

B: Chelsea

C: Fulham

D: Arsenal

52

On which continent are the Dolomite mountains?

A: Asia

B: Europe

C: Africa

D: Australia

53

Which character in the TV soap 'EastEnders' is played by Pam St Clement?

A: Melanie

B: Pat

C: Dot

D: Peggy

54

Scafell Pike is the highest point of which National Park?

A: Exmoor

B: Dartmoor

C: Northumberland

D: Lake District

55

For what is the Booker Prize awarded each year?

A: Art

B: Fashion

C: Fiction

D: Science

If you would like to use your 50:50 please turn to page 248
If you would like to Ask The Audience please turn to page 262
Turn to the answer section on page 272 to find out if you've won £8,000!

8 ◆ £8,000

56

Which month is named after a Roman emperor?

- A: January
- B: March
- C: June
- D: August

57

Morpheus was the Greek god of what?

- A: Love
- B: Peace
- C: War
- D: Sleep

58

Who starred in the film 'The Hustler'?

- A: Lee Marvin
- B: Steve McQueen
- C: Robert Redford
- D: Paul Newman

59

In which county is the city of Winchester?

- A: Somerset
- B: Hampshire
- C: Kent
- D: Norfolk

60

Who wrote the novel 'Barchester Towers'?

- A: Charles Dickens
- B: Anthony Trollope
- C: George Eliot
- D: Thomas Hardy

If you would like to use your 50:50 please turn to page 248
If you would like to Ask The Audience please turn to page 262
Turn to the answer section on page 272 to find out if you've won £8,000!

15		£1 MILLION
14		£500,000
13		£250,000
12		£125,000
11		£64,000
10		**£32,000**
9	◆	**£16,000**
8	◆	£8,000
7	◆	£4,000
6	◆	£2,000
5	◆	**£1,000**
4	◆	£500
3	◆	£300
2	◆	£200
1	◆	£100

1

In which year did the National Lottery commence in Britain?

A: 1992

B: 1993

C: 1994

D: 1995

2

In America, the name Hank is derived from which other name?

A: Herbert

B: Harrison

C: Henry

D: Hannibal

3

Who immediately follows Princess Eugenie in succession to the throne?

A: Prince Edward

B: Princess Beatrice

C: Princess Anne

D: Princess Margaret

4

Which word represents the last letter in the phonetic alphabet?

A: Zebra

B: Zulu

C: Zip

D: Zephyr

5

Which Russian word, meaning 'peace', was the name given to the Space Station launched in 1986?

A: Sputnik

B: Mir

C: Vostok

D: Soyuz

If you would like to use your 50:50 please turn to page 249
If you would like to Ask The Audience please turn to page 263
Turn to the answer section on page 273 to find out if you've won £16,000!

9 ◆ £16,000

6

What is the international car registration for Switzerland?

A: CS

B: CH

C: SN

D: SWA

7

The characters Lister and Rimmer appear in which TV sitcom?

A: The Brittas Empire

B: Red Dwarf

C: Brush Strokes

D: Men Behaving Badly

8

What kind of food is 'mascarpone'?

A: Cured meat

B: Natural yoghurt

C: Multi-grain bread

D: Soft cheese

9

Which Swiss resort hosts an annual television festival with the Golden Rose as the top award?

A: Geneva

B: Lausanne

C: Montreux

D: Lucerne

10

In which country is the port of Gdansk?

A: Russia

B: Netherlands

C: Hungary

D: Poland

If you would like to use your 50:50 please turn to page 249
If you would like to Ask The Audience please turn to page 263
Turn to the answer section on page 273 to find out if you've won £16,000!

11

Which of these pop groups have recorded the theme song to a James Bond film?

A: Duran Duran
B: B*Witched
C: Abba
D: Steps

12

Which craftsman uses a 'last' in his work?

A: Cobbler
B: Caddie
C: Cooper
D: Carpenter

13

Which of these cities has hosted an Olympic Games?

A: Madrid
B: Milan
C: Munich
D: Marseilles

14

In Greek mythology, where did the Minotaur live?

A: Sparta
B: Mycenae
C: Crete
D: Olympia

15

What is the specific name for the home of a beaver?

A: Warren
B: Lodge
C: Form
D: Sett

If you would like to use your 50:50 please turn to page 249
If you would like to Ask The Audience please turn to page 263
Turn to the answer section on page 273 to find out if you've won £16,000!

9 ♦ £16,000

16

Which famous novel ends with the words 'After all, tomorrow is another day'?

- A: Wuthering Heights
- B: Doctor Zhivago
- C: Nineteen Eighty-four
- D: Gone With The Wind

17

Of which country was Bob Hawke the prime minister from 1983 to 1991?

- A: Canada
- B: Australia
- C: New Zealand
- D: Jamaica

18

Which British composer co-founded the Promenade Concerts in 1895?

- A: Malcolm Sargent
- B: William Walton
- C: Henry Wood
- D: Arthur Sullivan

19

What type of bird is a greylag?

- A: Goose
- B: Swan
- C: Dove
- D: Duck

20

In which organ is insulin produced?

- A: Spleen
- B: Liver
- C: Pancreas
- D: Kidney

If you would like to use your 50:50 please turn to page 249
If you would like to Ask The Audience please turn to page 263
Turn to the answer section on page 273 to find out if you've won £16,000!

21

Who wrote the book 'Cider with Rosie'?

A: H.E. Bates
B: Laurie Lee
C: Somerset Maugham
D: D.H. Lawrence

22

Harare is the capital of which country?

A: Zimbabwe
B: Ghana
C: Libya
D: Liberia

23

Where in the human body is there a bone called the ulna?

A: Head
B: Leg
C: Arm
D: Ear

24

In which US state is Pearl Harbor?

A: California
B: Florida
C: Hawaii
D: Texas

25

Who wrote the novel 'Silas Marner'?

A: George Eliot
B: R.L. Stevenson
C: J.M. Barrie
D: Charles Dickens

If you would like to use your 50:50 please turn to page 249
If you would like to Ask The Audience please turn to page 263
Turn to the answer section on page 273 to find out if you've won £16,000!

26

Sofia is the capital of which country?

A: Algeria
B: Argentina
C: Bulgaria
D: Portugal

27

Where was singer Gloria Estefan born?

A: India
B: Great Britain
C: France
D: Cuba

28

In 'The Hunchback of Notre Dame', who befriends Quasimodo?

A: Estelle
B: Matilda
C: Alicia
D: Esmerelda

29

Which two colours form the national flag of Japan?

A: Blue and white
B: Red and blue
C: Red and white
D: Blue and gold

30

What name is given to the red and blue hazards on a skiing slalom course?

A: Jumps
B: Gates
C: Traps
D: Bunkers

If you would like to use your 50:50 please turn to page 249
If you would like to Ask The Audience please turn to page 263
Turn to the answer section on page 273 to find out if you've won £16,000!

9 ◆ £16,000

31

In which city is the Brandenburg Gate?

A: Berlin

B: Amsterdam

C: Antwerp

D: Oslo

32

What was President Hoover's first name?

A: Herbert

B: Woodrow

C: Calvin

D: Dwight

33

What nationality was the artist Goya?

A: French

B: Dutch

C: Spanish

D: Italian

34

With which profession is the Hippocratic oath associated?

A: Architects

B: Barristers

C: Doctors

D: Surveyors

35

What was the title of Steven Spielberg's film version of 'Peter Pan'?

A: Peter and Wendy

B: Neverland

C: Hook

D: The Lost Boys

If you would like to use your 50:50 please turn to page 249
If you would like to Ask The Audience please turn to page 263
Turn to the answer section on page 273 to find out if you've won £16,000!

36

What nationality was the racing driver Ayrton Senna?

A: Italian

B: Brazilian

C: Argentinian

D: French

37

Lake Garda is in which country?

A: France

B: Italy

C: Sweden

D: Canada

38

The Society of Friends is a formal name for which Christian sect?

A: Mormons

B: Quakers

C: Baptists

D: Methodists

39

In which sport is Mick the Miller a famous name?

A: Baseball

B: Greyhound racing

C: Pigeon racing

D: Wrestling

40

Which type of instrument is a marimba?

A: Keyboard

B: Brass

C: Woodwind

D: Percussion

If you would like to use your 50:50 please turn to page 249
If you would like to Ask The Audience please turn to page 263
Turn to the answer section on page 273 to find out if you've won £16,000!

9 ◆ £16,000

41

Who starred in the film 'Half A Sixpence'?

A: Danny Kaye
B: Tommy Steele
C: Fred Astaire
D: Gene Kelly

42

On which island was Napoleon Bonaparte born?

A: Sicily
B: Crete
C: Sardinia
D: Corsica

43

What is 'mal de mer'?

A: Homesickness
B: Carsickness
C: Airsickness
D: Seasickness

44

Ronald Reagan was Governor of which American state?

A: California
B: New York
C: Michigan
D: Florida

45

In which county is Epsom racecourse?

A: Surrey
B: Kent
C: Hampshire
D: West Sussex

If you would like to use your 50:50 please turn to page 249
If you would like to Ask The Audience please turn to page 263
Turn to the answer section on page 273 to find out if you've won £16,000!

46

The Great Red Spot is a feature of which planet?

- A: Venus
- B: Neptune
- C: Jupiter
- D: Pluto

47

Norman Foster is a famous name in which field?

- A: Astronomy
- B: Music
- C: Mathematics
- D: Architecture

48

In which city is De Montfort University?

- A: Glasgow
- B: Manchester
- C: Leicester
- D: Bristol

49

Which of these is a measure of mineral hardness?

- A: Celsius
- B: Beaufort
- C: Mohs
- D: Richter

50

Vancouver is in which Canadian province?

- A: British Columbia
- B: Alberta
- C: Quebec
- D: Ontario

If you would like to use your 50:50 please turn to page 249
If you would like to Ask The Audience please turn to page 263
Turn to the answer section on page 273 to find out if you've won £16,000!

51

With which sport is Jack Hobbs associated?

A: Golf

B: Cricket

C: Rugby union

D: Tennis

52

On which continent is Lake Titicaca?

A: South America

B: Australia

C: Africa

D: Asia

53

What is a sampan?

A: Fish

B: Boat

C: Shoe

D: Hat

54

In which century was the English Civil War fought?

A: 13th

B: 15th

C: 17th

D: 19th

55

In which decade was the Festival of Britain held?

A: 1940s

B: 1950s

C: 1960s

D: 1970s

If you would like to use your 50:50 please turn to page 249
If you would like to Ask The Audience please turn to page 263
Turn to the answer section on page 273 to find out if you've won £16,000!

56

The Reverend W. Awdry created which character?

A: Rupert Bear

B: Thomas the Tank Engine

C: Winnie-the-Pooh

D: Mr Toad

If you would like to use your 50:50 please turn to page 249
If you would like to Ask The Audience please turn to page 263
Turn to the answer section on page 273 to find out if you've won £16,000!

15	£1 MILLION
14	£500,000
13	£250,000
12	£125,000
11	£64,000
10 ◆	**£32,000**
9 ◆	£16,000
8 ◆	£8,000
7 ◆	£4,000
6 ◆	£2,000
5 ◆	**£1,000**
4 ◆	£500
3 ◆	£300
2 ◆	£200
1 ◆	£100

1

Who were Dicky Mint, Mick the Marmaliser and Nigel Ponsonby-Smallpiece?

A: Diddymen

B: Wombles

C: Pogles

D: Clangers

2

Who composed the opera 'The Magic Flute'?

A: Verdi

B: Mozart

C: Puccini

D: Wagner

3

Khartoum is the capital of which country?

A: Nepal

B: Ghana

C: Vietnam

D: Sudan

4

The tympanic membrane is the medical name for which part of the body?

A: Diaphragm

B: Vocal cord

C: Eardrum

D: Heart valve

5

Which actress starred in the films 'Ninotchka' and 'Grand Hotel'?

A: Greta Garbo

B: Katharine Hepburn

C: Ginger Rogers

D: Rita Hayworth

If you would like to use your 50:50 please turn to page 250
If you would like to Ask The Audience please turn to page 264
Turn to the answer section on page 273 to find out if you've won £32,000!

6

The Farne Islands are in which sea?

A: Irish Sea
B: North Sea
C: Bay of Biscay
D: Baltic Sea

7

Which prime minister took Britain into the European Common Market?

A: Harold Wilson
B: Edward Heath
C: James Callaghan
D: Margaret Thatcher

8

In which mythology was Anubis a god?

A: Roman
B: Greek
C: Norse
D: Egyptian

9

Novelist Clare Francis first found fame in which field?

A: Gardening
B: Cooking
C: Sailing
D: Acting

10

What is the principal religion of Algeria?

A: Christianity
B: Islam
C: Hinduism
D: Judaism

If you would like to use your 50:50 please turn to page 250
If you would like to Ask The Audience please turn to page 264
Turn to the answer section on page 273 to find out if you've won £32,000!

11

Which of these dames was a famous singer?

- A: Margot Fonteyn
- B: Clara Butt
- C: Edith Evans
- D: Agatha Christie

12

Which Latin word means 'let it stand'?

- A: Alibi
- B: Mensa
- C: Alias
- D: Stet

13

Paul Hewson is the real name of which popular singer?

- A: Fish
- B: Sting
- C: Bono
- D: Suggs

14

Tabasco is a state in which country?

- A: Italy
- B: Hungary
- C: Mexico
- D: Pakistan

15

Who composed the oratorio 'The Creation'?

- A: Holst
- B: Offenbach
- C: Bizet
- D: Haydn

If you would like to use your 50:50 please turn to page 250
If you would like to Ask The Audience please turn to page 264
Turn to the answer section on page 273 to find out if you've won £32,000!

16

Which prime minister became the Earl of Stockton?

A: Alec Douglas-Home

B: Harold Macmillan

C: Stanley Baldwin

D: Clement Attlee

17

Which town is the administrative headquarters of Cornwall?

A: Truro

B: Yeovil

C: Taunton

D: Ilfracombe

18

What was the first name of the painter J.M.W. Turner?

A: Joseph

B: Jeremy

C: Joshua

D: Julian

19

What is the official language of San Marino?

A: Italian

B: Spanish

C: French

D: German

20

Who was the first US president to visit China while in office?

A: Bush

B: Clinton

C: Carter

D: Nixon

If you would like to use your 50:50 please turn to page 250
If you would like to Ask The Audience please turn to page 264
Turn to the answer section on page 273 to find out if you've won £32,000!

21

Which author created the character Hannibal Lecter?

A: Thomas Harris
B: Patricia Cornwell
C: Joseph Heller
D: Robert Ludlum

22

What nationality was the navigator Abel Tasman?

A: German
B: Swedish
C: Dutch
D: Spanish

23

In which of these films did
Fred Astaire dance with Cyd Charisse?

A: Brigadoon
B: Top Hat
C: The Band Wagon
D: Singin' In The Rain

24

In which British city is St Mungo's Cathedral?

A: Birmingham
B: Canterbury
C: Durham
D: Glasgow

25

A calorie is a unit of what?

A: Light
B: Heat
C: Resistance
D: Sound

If you would like to use your 50:50 please turn to page 250
If you would like to Ask The Audience please turn to page 264
Turn to the answer section on page 273 to find out if you've won £32,000!

26

What colour is the pigment sepia?

A: Brown
B: Green
C: Blue
D: Yellow

27

Which of these musical terms means 'gradually getting louder'?

A: Adagio
B: Crescendo
C: Lento
D: Piano

28

Which US president displayed on his desk a sign which read "The buck stops here"?

A: Harry S. Truman
B: Richard Nixon
C: Jimmy Carter
D: Franklin D. Roosevelt

29

Who wrote the children's story 'The Railway Children'?

A: E. Nesbit
B: R.L. Stevenson
C: J.R.R. Tolkien
D: J.K. Rowling

30

Who was the Queen consort to King George V?

A: Mary
B: Alexandra
C: Adelaide
D: Charlotte

If you would like to use your 50:50 please turn to page 250
If you would like to Ask The Audience please turn to page 264
Turn to the answer section on page 273 to find out if you've won £32,000!

10 ◆ £32,000

31

During which war was the Victoria Cross instituted?

A: American Civil War
B: Crimean War
C: World War Two
D: Napoleonic War

32

In which county is Longleat House?

A: Wiltshire
B: Gloucestershire
C: Sussex
D: Hampshire

33

Declan McManus is the real name of which famous pop singer?

A: Sting
B: Tom Jones
C: Elvis Costello
D: David Bowie

34

In which field of the arts was Barbara Hepworth a famous name?

A: Porcelain
B: Opera
C: Sculpture
D: Ballet

35

Which famous sailor was killed in 1805?

A: Nelson
B: Drake
C: Cook
D: Raleigh

If you would like to use your 50:50 please turn to page 250
If you would like to Ask The Audience please turn to page 264
Turn to the answer section on page 273 to find out if you've won £32,000!

10 ♦ £32,000

36

K is the chemical symbol for which element?

A: Krypton

B: Plutonium

C: Argon

D: Potassium

37

Which fish gives its name to a patterning of the sky?

A: Tuna

B: Haddock

C: Trout

D: Mackerel

38

Which actress starred in the film 'The Blue Angel'?

A: Bette Davis

B: Marilyn Monroe

C: Marlene Dietrich

D: Judy Garland

39

What was the surname of the bank robber Clyde, of Bonnie and Clyde fame?

A: Barrie

B: Barron

C: Barrett

D: Barrow

40

Who wrote the musical 'Blood Brothers'?

A: Alan Bleasdale

B: Lionel Bart

C: Willy Russell

D: Anthony Newley

If you would like to use your 50:50 please turn to page 250
If you would like to Ask The Audience please turn to page 264
Turn to the answer section on page 273 to find out if you've won £32,000!

41

In which country is Farsi the official language?

A: Iraq

B: Greece

C: Philippines

D: Iran

42

Which oil billionaire used his fortune to found a museum of art in California?

A: Nelson Rockefeller

B: John Paul Getty

C: Barry Goldwater

D: George Bush

43

In mythology, what kind of creature was Medusa?

A: Cyclops

B: Siren

C: Muse

D: Gorgon

44

In which country was the Aztec Empire based?

A: Bolivia

B: Peru

C: Ecuador

D: Mexico

45

Thomas Minton was best known for making what?

A: Porcelain

B: Furniture

C: Confectionery

D: Glassware

If you would like to use your 50:50 please turn to page 250
If you would like to Ask The Audience please turn to page 264
Turn to the answer section on page 273 to find out if you've won £32,000!

46

Where did Florence Nightingale set up a hospital to tend the wounded of the Crimean War?

A: Alexandria
B: Darjeeling
C: Scutari
D: Constantinople

47

Which poet married the author of 'Frankenstein'?

A: John Keats
B: William Wordsworth
C: Percy Bysshe Shelley
D: Lord Byron

48

At which racecourse is the Oaks run?

A: Ascot
B: Epsom
C: Cheltenham
D: Newmarket

49

Which musical features the song 'Love Changes Everything'?

A: Miss Saigon
B: Les Misérables
C: Evita
D: Aspects of Love

50

What type of creature is a redpoll?

A: Butterfly
B: Bird
C: Crab
D: Beetle

If you would like to use your 50:50 please turn to page 250
If you would like to Ask The Audience please turn to page 264
Turn to the answer section on page 273 to find out if you've won £32,000!

51

Which of these islands is situated south of the equator?

A: Sri Lanka

B: Madagascar

C: Cuba

D: Trinidad

52

Cheddar Gorge is in which range of hills?

A: Mendips

B: Chilterns

C: Malverns

D: Cheviots

If you would like to use your 50:50 please turn to page 250
If you would like to Ask The Audience please turn to page 264
Turn to the answer section on page 273 to find out if you've won £32,000!

15	£1 MILLION
14	£500,000
13	£250,000
12	£125,000
11 ◆	**£64,000**
10 ◆	**£32,000**
9 ◆	£16,000
8 ◆	£8,000
7 ◆	£4,000
6 ◆	£2,000
5 ◆	**£1,000**
4 ◆	£500
3 ◆	£300
2 ◆	£200
1 ◆	£100

1

Which prime minister had a wife called Clementine?

A: Churchill

B: Eden

C: Baldwin

D: Macmillan

2

What is the Japanese 'Shinkansen'?

A: Main meal of the day

B: Large dolphin

C: High speed train

D: Traditional headdress

3

In which country are the Drakensberg mountains?

A: New Zealand

B: South Africa

C: Greenland

D: Austria

4

How many points are awarded for coming third in a Formula One Grand Prix?

A: Six

B: Five

C: Four

D: Three

5

Who is the President of the World Wide Fund for Nature?

A: Duke of Edinburgh

B: Duke of Kent

C: Duke of Gloucester

D: Duke of York

If you would like to use your 50:50 please turn to page 251
If you would like to Ask The Audience please turn to page 265
Turn to the answer section on page 273 to find out if you've won £64,000!

6

Who wrote the play 'What the Butler Saw'?

A: Joe Orton

B: Harold Pinter

C: John Osborne

D: Tom Stoppard

7

Whose official residence is the Mansion House?

A: Home Secretary

B: Lord Mayor of London

C: Lord Chancellor

D: Bishop of London

8

In which century was the Battle of Bannockburn fought?

A: 14th

B: 15th

C: 16th

D: 17th

9

Who wrote the poem 'The Tyger'?

A: Coleridge

B: Blake

C: Shelley

D: Wordsworth

10

The city of Gloucester lies on which river?

A: Ouse

B: Severn

C: Trent

D: Wye

If you would like to use your 50:50 please turn to page 251
If you would like to Ask The Audience please turn to page 265
Turn to the answer section on page 273 to find out if you've won £64,000!

11

Which crop is affected by the boll weevil?

- ◆A: Potato
- ◆B: Tea
- ◆C: Grape
- ◆D: Cotton

12

What is an 'ouzel'?

- ◆A: Bird
- ◆B: Reptile
- ◆C: Fish
- ◆D: Insect

13

Who created the clerical detective Father Brown?

- ◆A: G.K. Chesterton
- ◆B: Dorothy L. Sayers
- ◆C: Leslie Charteris
- ◆D: Ruth Rendell

14

The dodo was native to which island?

- ◆A: Mauritius
- ◆B: Borneo
- ◆C: Zanzibar
- ◆D: Madagascar

15

What was the profession of John Maynard Keynes?

- ◆A: Clergyman
- ◆B: Economist
- ◆C: Mountaineer
- ◆D: Soldier

If you would like to use your 50:50 please turn to page 251
If you would like to Ask The Audience please turn to page 265
Turn to the answer section on page 273 to find out if you've won £64,000!

16

Which major desert lies in Mongolia and China?

- A: Atacama
- B: Gibson
- C: Kalahari
- D: Gobi

17

Who was the last emperor of Germany?

- A: Wilhelm
- B: Otto
- C: Franz
- D: Joseph

18

Who is the mother of Lord Linley and Lady Sarah Chatto?

- A: Princess Alexandra
- B: Princess Anne
- C: Princess Michael
- D: Princess Margaret

19

Who wrote the novel 'To Kill a Mockingbird'?

- A: Harper Lee
- B: Norman Mailer
- C: James Clavell
- D: William Faulkner

20

What is the internationally accepted basic unit of time?

- A: Second
- B: Minute
- C: Hour
- D: Day

If you would like to use your 50:50 please turn to page 251
If you would like to Ask The Audience please turn to page 265
Turn to the answer section on page 273 to find out if you've won £64,000!

21

The name of which chemical element is derived from the Greek word for 'sun'?

- A: Radon
- B: Helium
- C: Argon
- D: Oxygen

22

What is Rumpole of the Bailey's first name?

- A: Horace
- B: Harold
- C: Hector
- D: Herbert

23

In computing, what is the name of the line of text printed at the bottom of each page?

- A: Footer
- B: Header
- C: Glossary
- D: Baseline

24

Which is the longest river in France?

- A: Seine
- B: Loire
- C: Rhône
- D: Garonne

25

Who succeeded Harold Wilson as leader of the Labour Party?

- A: Neil Kinnock
- B: Michael Foot
- C: John Smith
- D: James Callaghan

If you would like to use your 50:50 please turn to page 251
If you would like to Ask The Audience please turn to page 265
Turn to the answer section on page 273 to find out if you've won £64,000!

11 ♦ £64,000

26

Who is credited with inventing the lightning-conductor?

A: Abraham Lincoln

B: George Washington

C: Benjamin Franklin

D: Thomas Jefferson

27

Elaine, Jerry, George and Kramer
are characters in which TV sitcom?

A: The Larry Sanders Show

B: Frasier

C: Seinfeld

D: Caroline in the City

28

Which organisation has a symbol of a
globe flanked by two olive branches?

A: NATO

B: United Nations

C: Organization of African Unity

D: Commonwealth

29

What is the name for a university department
which offers a particular area of study?

A: Chapter

B: Division

C: Unit

D: Faculty

30

Which bird's pink plumage is
derived from pigments in its food?

A: Macaw

B: Bullfinch

C: Flamingo

D: Pelican

If you would like to use your 50:50 please turn to page 251
If you would like to Ask The Audience please turn to page 265
Turn to the answer section on page 273 to find out if you've won £64,000!

31

The World Series is a contest in which sport?

A: Basketball

B: American football

C: Ice hockey

D: Baseball

32

A Monégasque is a native of which country?

A: Mongolia

B: Madagascar

C: Monaco

D: Malta

33

Who directed the film 'Doctor Zhivago'?

A: David Lean

B: Robert Wise

C: Carol Reed

D: Billy Wilder

34

What type of teeth are wisdom teeth?

A: Incisor

B: Canine

C: Milk

D: Molar

35

Kevin Keegan was in charge of which football team when he became England manager?

A: Fulham

B: Charlton Athletic

C: West Ham United

D: Crystal Palace

If you would like to use your 50:50 please turn to page 251
If you would like to Ask The Audience please turn to page 265
Turn to the answer section on page 273 to find out if you've won £64,000!

36

In which county is the port of Gravesend?

A: Essex
B: Kent
C: West Sussex
D: East Sussex

37

Desdemona is a character in which Shakespeare play?

A: Othello
B: Macbeth
C: Hamlet
D: King Lear

38

Who gave his name to a cricketing almanac?

A: Whitaker
B: Wisden
C: Debrett
D: Burke

39

Who wrote the children's story 'The Borrowers'?

A: Enid Blyton
B: Mary Norton
C: E. Nesbit
D: Beatrix Potter

40

In which American state is the Napa Valley?

A: Oregon
B: Florida
C: Nevada
D: California

If you would like to use your 50:50 please turn to page 251
If you would like to Ask The Audience please turn to page 265
Turn to the answer section on page 273 to find out if you've won £64,000!

41

What is the number of Beethoven's 'Choral' Symphony?

A: Third
B: Fifth
C: Seventh
D: Ninth

42

What was the venue of the 1976 Summer Olympic Games?

A: Moscow
B: Montreal
C: Melbourne
D: Mexico City

43

Who was married to US comedian George Burns?

A: Gracie Allen
B: Lucille Ball
C: Gloria Swanson
D: Ethel Merman

44

Jeremy Thorpe was the leader of which political party?

A: Liberal
B: Labour
C: Conservative
D: SDP

45

Who wrote the play 'Under Milk Wood'?

A: Dylan Thomas
B: T.S. Eliot
C: Wilfred Owen
D: Rupert Brooke

If you would like to use your 50:50 please turn to page 251
If you would like to Ask The Audience please turn to page 265
Turn to the answer section on page 273 to find out if you've won £64,000!

46

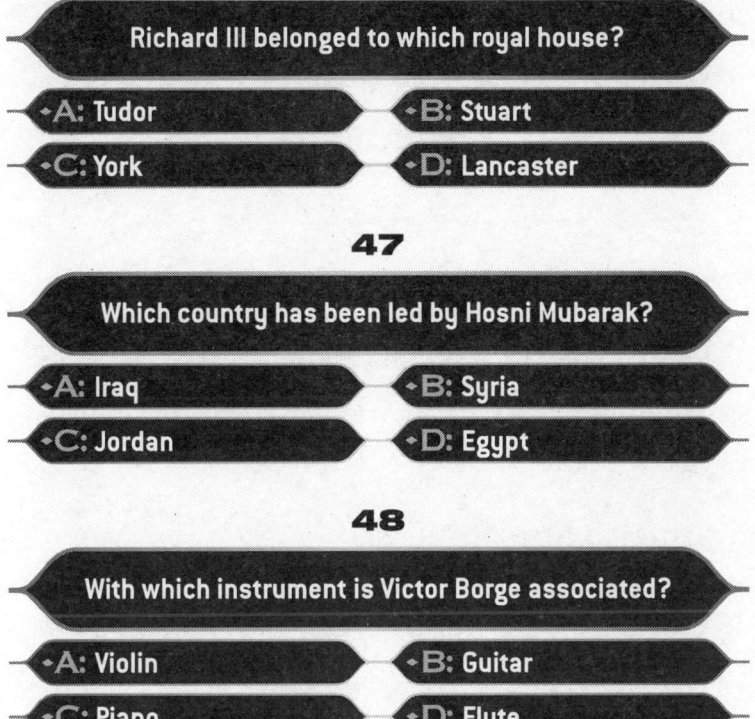

Richard III belonged to which royal house?

A: Tudor
B: Stuart
C: York
D: Lancaster

47

Which country has been led by Hosni Mubarak?

A: Iraq
B: Syria
C: Jordan
D: Egypt

48

With which instrument is Victor Borge associated?

A: Violin
B: Guitar
C: Piano
D: Flute

If you would like to use your 50:50 please turn to page 251
If you would like to Ask The Audience please turn to page 265
Turn to the answer section on page 273 to find out if you've won £64,000!

15	£1 MILLION
14	£500,000
13	£250,000
12 ♦	**£125,000**
11 ♦	£64,000
10 ♦	**£32,000**
9 ♦	£16,000
8 ♦	£8,000
7 ♦	£4,000
6 ♦	£2,000
5 ♦	**£1,000**
4 ♦	£500
3 ♦	£300
2 ♦	£200
1 ♦	£100

1

The word 'safari' means 'journey' in which language?

A: Hindi
B: Turkish
C: Persian
D: Swahili

2

Baffin Island is part of which country?

A: Canada
B: Norway
C: Iceland
D: Chile

3

Who did Jack Straw succeed as Home Secretary?

A: Michael Howard
B: Kenneth Clarke
C: Michael Portillo
D: Douglas Hurd

4

What is the common name for
the chemical potassium nitrate?

A: Baking powder
B: Epsom salts
C: Bleach
D: Saltpetre

5

What nationality is Boutros Boutros-Ghali,
UN Secretary General from 1992 to 1997?

A: Ghanaian
B: Finnish
C: Egyptian
D: Peruvian

If you would like to use your 50:50 please turn to page 252
If you would like to Ask The Audience please turn to page 266
Turn to the answer section on page 274 to find out if you've won £125,000!

12 ◆ £125,000

6

Who wrote the song 'I Will Always Love You', a hit in 1992 for Whitney Houston?

- **A: Henry Mancini**
- **B: Burt Bacharach**
- **C: Don Black**
- **D: Dolly Parton**

7

Which European language is officially used in Madagascar?

- **A: French**
- **B: Spanish**
- **C: Dutch**
- **D: Italian**

8

Humphrey Bogart won his Best Actor Oscar for which film?

- **A: The African Queen**
- **B: Casablanca**
- **C: The Maltese Falcon**
- **D: The Big Sleep**

9

Who fought Rome in the Punic Wars?

- **A: Carthage**
- **B: Gaul**
- **C: Sparta**
- **D: Egypt**

10

What was the name of the first US space shuttle?

- **A: Discovery**
- **B: Columbia**
- **C: Challenger**
- **D: Atlantis**

If you would like to use your 50:50 please turn to page 252
If you would like to Ask The Audience please turn to page 266
Turn to the answer section on page 274 to find out if you've won £125,000!

11

Quark is a type of which food?

A: Cheese

B: Bread

C: Sausage

D: Butter

12

Casablanca is in which country?

A: Algeria

B: Tunisia

C: Morocco

D: Egypt

13

Frederick the Great was king of which country?

A: Luxembourg

B: Prussia

C: Burgundy

D: Flanders

14

Which river flows through the Grand Canyon?

A: Missouri

B: Colorado

C: Hudson

D: Rio Grande

15

Which empire was ruled by Genghis Khan?

A: Persian

B: Mongol

C: Japanese

D: Byzantine

If you would like to use your 50:50 please turn to page 252
If you would like to Ask The Audience please turn to page 266
Turn to the answer section on page 274 to find out if you've won £125,000!

12 ◆ £125,000

16

In which sport was Mary Peters an Olympic gold medallist?

A: Gymnastics
B: Athletics
C: Swimming
D: Judo

17

Who wrote the music for 'West Side Story'?

A: Stephen Sondheim
B: George Gershwin
C: Leonard Bernstein
D: Richard Rodgers

18

Haematite is the main ore of which metal?

A: Aluminium
B: Mercury
C: Lead
D: Iron

19

Which Formula One Grand Prix takes place at the Spa circuit?

A: German
B: Austrian
C: Belgian
D: Hungarian

20

What was the first name of the composer Mahler?

A: Gustav
B: Joseph
C: Hans
D: Henrik

If you would like to use your 50:50 please turn to page 252
If you would like to Ask The Audience please turn to page 266
Turn to the answer section on page 274 to find out if you've won £125,000!

12 ◆ £125,000

21

Who presides over the House of Lords?

A: Lord Chamberlain

B: Lord Commissioner

C: Lord Chief Justice

D: Lord Chancellor

22

The Dominican Republic is situated on which island?

A: Hispaniola

B: Puerto Rico

C: Cuba

D: Dominica

23

The decompression sickness 'the bends' is caused by bubbles of which gas?

A: Nitrogen

B: Hydrogen

C: Oxygen

D: Carbon dioxide

24

Which of these US presidents was a Democrat?

A: Bush

B: Carter

C: Ford

D: Eisenhower

25

With which athletics event is Bob Beamon associated?

A: Triple jump

B: Pole vault

C: Long jump

D: Javelin

If you would like to use your 50:50 please turn to page 252
If you would like to Ask The Audience please turn to page 266
Turn to the answer section on page 274 to find out if you've won £125,000!

26

What type of bird is a 'lory'?

A: Pigeon

B: Duck

C: Parrot

D: Eagle

27

In which city is the Bodleian Library?

A: Cambridge

B: Edinburgh

C: London

D: Oxford

28

In George Orwell's 'Animal Farm', what kind of creature is Napoleon?

A: Horse

B: Cow

C: Pig

D: Sheep

29

Which national daily newspaper was founded in Manchester in 1821?

A: Daily Express

B: Daily Telegraph

C: Guardian

D: Times

30

Traditionally, pewter was a blend of tin and which other metal?

A: Copper

B: Lead

C: Silver

D: Iron

If you would like to use your 50:50 please turn to page 252
If you would like to Ask The Audience please turn to page 266
Turn to the answer section on page 274 to find out if you've won £125,000!

31

Who provides the voice of Chef in the TV cartoon series 'South Park'?

A: Barry White

B: Isaac Hayes

C: Smokey Robinson

D: Errol Brown

32

Which American city forms a metropolitan area with Dallas?

A: Houston

B: San Antonio

C: Austin

D: Fort Worth

33

'Slippery When Wet' was a hit album for which rock band?

A: Guns N' Roses

B: Whitesnake

C: Bon Jovi

D: Aerosmith

34

Which metal is obtained from bauxite?

A: Aluminium

B: Sodium

C: Copper

D: Tin

35

What kind of animal is a 'Jacob'?

A: Pig

B: Goat

C: Horse

D: Sheep

If you would like to use your 50:50 please turn to page 252
If you would like to Ask The Audience please turn to page 266
Turn to the answer section on page 274 to find out if you've won £125,000!

36

Which Shakespeare play is set in the forest of Arden?

A: As You Like It

B: Twelfth Night

C: Measure For Measure

D: A Midsummer Night's Dream

37

In which country are the ruins of Carthage?

A: Libya

B: Tunisia

C: Turkey

D: Jordan

38

With which form of transport is Igor Sikorsky most associated?

A: Hovercraft

B: Helicopter

C: Submarine

D: Motorcycle

39

What name is given to the study of insects?

A: Entomology

B: Potamology

C: Gastrology

D: Nephrology

40

The Victoria Falls separate Zimbabwe from which other country?

A: Swaziland

B: Zambia

C: Botswana

D: Mozambique

If you would like to use your 50:50 please turn to page 252
If you would like to Ask The Audience please turn to page 266
Turn to the answer section on page 274 to find out if you've won £125,000!

12 ◆ £125,000

41

With which instrument was
Andrés Segovia most associated?

A: Cello

B: Piano

C: Violin

D: Guitar

42

What is the official language of Zambia?

A: English

B: French

C: Spanish

D: Portuguese

43

Which garden flower has the Latin name 'Helianthus'?

A: Marigold

B: Dahlia

C: Petunia

D: Sunflower

44

Brunei is on which island?

A: Hispaniola

B: Java

C: New Guinea

D: Borneo

If you would like to use your 50:50 please turn to page 252
If you would like to Ask The Audience please turn to page 266
Turn to the answer section on page 274 to find out if you've won £125,000!

15	£1 MILLION
14	£500,000
13 ◆	**£250,000**
12 ◆	£125,000
11 ◆	£64,000
10 ◆	**£32,000**
9 ◆	£16,000
8 ◆	£8,000
7 ◆	£4,000
6 ◆	£2,000
5 ◆	**£1,000**
4 ◆	£500
3 ◆	£300
2 ◆	£200
1 ◆	£100

1

Cagliari is the capital of which island?

A: Sardinia

B: Capri

C: Sicily

D: Elba

2

Which country won the most gold medals at the Atlanta Olympics?

A: Russia

B: Germany

C: China

D: USA

3

What is an avocet?

A: Bird

B: Fruit

C: Musical instrument

D: Tool

4

What does the letter C stand for in the acronym UNICEF?

A: Community

B: Citizens

C: Commission

D: Children's

5

What is the largest lake in Africa?

A: Tanganyika

B: Victoria

C: Chad

D: Nasser

If you would like to use your 50:50 please turn to page 253
If you would like to Ask The Audience please turn to page 267
Turn to the answer section on page 274 to find out if you've won £250,000!

6

Where was film director Ingmar Bergman born?

- ◆A: Germany
- ◆B: Denmark
- ◆C: Norway
- ◆D: Sweden

7

Who was the Roman goddess of hunting?

- ◆A: Diana
- ◆B: Vesta
- ◆C: Pomona
- ◆D: Victoria

8

Erich Honecker was a notorious leader of which country?

- ◆A: Czechoslovakia
- ◆B: Romania
- ◆C: Hungary
- ◆D: East Germany

9

In the film 'Little Voice', who played the title character's mother?

- ◆A: Pauline Collins
- ◆B: Brenda Blethyn
- ◆C: Julie Walters
- ◆D: Alison Steadman

10

Which of these British cities is farthest west?

- ◆A: Chester
- ◆B: Bath
- ◆C: Cardiff
- ◆D: Liverpool

If you would like to use your 50:50 please turn to page 253
If you would like to Ask The Audience please turn to page 267
Turn to the answer section on page 274 to find out if you've won £250,000!

11

From where does Prince Charles derive his income?

A: The Queen

B: Duchy of Cornwall

C: The Treasury

D: Duchy of Lancaster

12

Which character did Jodie Foster play in the film 'Bugsy Malone'?

A: Clemenza

B: Sugar

C: Tallulah

D: Chickadee

13

Handel composed 'The Water Music' for a boating party held by which British king?

A: George I

B: George II

C: George III

D: George IV

14

Tallinn is the capital of which country?

A: Latvia

B: Estonia

C: Lithuania

D: Georgia

15

Where was the actor Omar Sharif born?

A: Jordan

B: Syria

C: Lebanon

D: Egypt

If you would like to use your 50:50 please turn to page 253
If you would like to Ask The Audience please turn to page 267
Turn to the answer section on page 274 to find out if you've won £250,000!

16

The 'clumber' is what type of dog?

A: Spaniel
B: Terrier
C: Labrador
D: Corgi

17

Springfield is the capital of which American state?

A: Illinois
B: Michigan
C: Missouri
D: Ohio

18

In the Bible, which book follows the four Gospels?

A: Romans
B: Acts
C: Kings
D: Numbers

19

Grunge music originated in which American city?

A: Seattle
B: Pittsburgh
C: Detroit
D: Boston

20

The word 'bungalow' comes from which language?

A: Hindi
B: Hebrew
C: Arabic
D: Swahili

If you would like to use your 50:50 please turn to page 253
If you would like to Ask The Audience please turn to page 267
Turn to the answer section on page 274 to find out if you've won £250,000!

21

Minsk, a city of the former Soviet Union, is now the capital of which country?

A: Belarus
B: Kazakhstan
C: Armenia
D: Lithuania

22

Cranwell military college trains personnel for which of the services?

A: Police
B: Army
C: Royal Navy
D: Royal Air Force

23

How many stars are there on the national flag of China?

A: Four
B: Five
C: Six
D: Seven

24

An 'erg' is a unit of what?

A: Volume
B: Mass
C: Pressure
D: Energy

25

Who succeeded Cecil Day-Lewis as Poet Laureate?

A: Alfred Austin
B: John Masefield
C: John Betjeman
D: Ted Hughes

If you would like to use your 50:50 please turn to page 253
If you would like to Ask The Audience please turn to page 267
Turn to the answer section on page 274 to find out if you've won £250,000!

26

In Greek mythology, Penelope was the faithful wife of which hero?

- A: Jason
- B: Achilles
- C: Odysseus
- D: Hector

27

Who was the second Roman emperor?

- A: Claudius
- B: Tiberius
- C: Nero
- D: Augustus

28

Where are the Mountains of Mourne?

- A: Northern Ireland
- B: Scotland
- C: England
- D: Wales

29

What was the French Gobelin factory famous for making?

- A: Porcelain
- B: Tapestries
- C: Glass
- D: Perfume

30

Who composed the opera 'Lohengrin'?

- A: Mahler
- B: Puccini
- C: Wagner
- D: Rossini

If you would like to use your 50:50 please turn to page 253
If you would like to Ask The Audience please turn to page 267
Turn to the answer section on page 274 to find out if you've won £250,000!

31

Frank Lloyd Wright designed
which famous New York building?

A: UN Headquarters
B: The Twin Towers
C: Empire State Building
D: Guggenheim Museum

32

Which of these Italian cities lies on the river Arno?

A: Florence
B: Milan
C: Rome
D: Venice

33

What is the SI unit of resistance?

A: Newton
B: Ohm
C: Farad
D: Joule

34

Who is the patron saint of music?

A: Bridget
B: Clare
C: Cecilia
D: Winifred

35

Which official represents the Crown in a British colony?

A: Chief Minister
B: Sheriff
C: Governor
D: Equerry

If you would like to use your 50:50 please turn to page 253
If you would like to Ask The Audience please turn to page 267
Turn to the answer section on page 274 to find out if you've won £250,000!

36

Which US city is served by Logan airport?

A: Chicago

B: Boston

C: New York

D: Los Angeles

37

What colour is the mineral malachite?

A: Black

B: White

C: Purple

D: Green

38

What is the title of Beethoven's only opera?

A: Aida

B: Fidelio

C: Salome

D: Turandot

39

Which English king was one of the 'Princes in the Tower'?

A: Charles II

B: William III

C: Henry IV

D: Edward V

40

Yellowstone National Park is mainly in which US state?

A: North Dakota

B: Kansas

C: Wyoming

D: Nevada

If you would like to use your 50:50 please turn to page 253
If you would like to Ask The Audience please turn to page 267
Turn to the answer section on page 274 to find out if you've won £250,000!

15   £1 MILLION

14 ◆ £500,000

13 ◆ £250,000

12 ◆ £125,000

11 ◆ £64,000

10 ◆ £32,000

9 ◆ £16,000

8 ◆ £8,000

7 ◆ £4,000

6 ◆ £2,000

5 ◆ £1,000

4 ◆ £500

3 ◆ £300

2 ◆ £200

1 ◆ £100

1

Which state was divided from Pennsylvania by the Mason-Dixon Line?

◆A: New York

B: Ohio

◆C: West Virginia

D: Maryland

2

Which artistic movement was founded by Tristan Tzara?

◆A: Art Deco

B: Surrealism

◆C: Dada

D: Cubism

3

The MP Jennie Lee was the wife of which Labour politician?

◆A: Aneurin Bevan

◆B: Ernest Bevin

◆C: Herbert Morrison

◆D: Clement Attlee

4

Which German author wrote 'All Quiet on the Western Front'?

◆A: Rainer Maria Rilke

◆B: Bertolt Brecht

◆C: Günter Grass

◆D: Erich Maria Remarque

5

The alphabet used in Russia is named after which saint?

◆A: Barnabus

◆B: Justinian

◆C: Cyril

◆D: Gregory

If you would like to use your 50:50 please turn to page 254
If you would like to Ask The Audience please turn to page 267
Turn to the answer section on page 274 to find out if you've won £500,000!

6

What was discovered by Joseph John Thomson in 1897?

- A: Neutron
- B: Nuclear fission
- C: Osmosis
- D: Electron

7

The 'kinkajou' belongs to which family of animals?

- A: Weasel
- B: Raccoon
- C: Deer
- D: Shrew

8

Martin Ryle was a holder of which post?

- A: Poet Laureate
- B: Astronomer Royal
- C: Archbishop of Canterbury
- D: Black Rod

9

What does 'c' refer to, in the famous theorem and mathematical formula $a^2 + b^2 = c^2$?

- A: Perpendicular
- B: Diameter
- C: Perimeter
- D: Hypotenuse

10

Which of these years will be a leap year?

- A: 2100
- B: 2200
- C: 2300
- D: 2400

If you would like to use your 50:50 please turn to page 254
If you would like to Ask The Audience please turn to page 267
Turn to the answer section on page 274 to find out if you've won £500,000!

11

Which of these people had the middle name 'Schwenck'?

- A: L.S. Lowry
- B: Harry S. Truman
- C: Arthur S. Sullivan
- D: William S. Gilbert

12

What is the Hindu Kush?

- A: Religious book
- B: Ceremonial dance
- C: Range of mountains
- D: National costume

13

In the New Testament, who is the sister of Lazarus and Mary?

- A: Salome
- B: Martha
- C: Esther
- D: Ruth

14

What do the initials stand for in the name of the author H.G. Wells?

- A: Horace George
- B: Herbert George
- C: Harold Gilbert
- D: Henry Gilbert

15

What is the official language of Guyana?

- A: Spanish
- B: Portuguese
- C: French
- D: English

If you would like to use your 50:50 please turn to page 254
If you would like to Ask The Audience please turn to page 267
Turn to the answer section on page 274 to find out if you've won £500,000!

14 ◆ £500,000

16

Which of these politicians resigned
from the cabinet in 1990?

A: Leon Brittan

B: Michael Heseltine

C: Geoffrey Howe

D: Nigel Lawson

17

Which European country's national flag has
horizontal stripes of red, white and light blue?

A: France

B: Belgium

C: Luxembourg

D: Austria

18

Which of these is the name of a
city in both Libya and Lebanon?

A: Beirut

B: Sidon

C: Tripoli

D: Benghazi

19

In which year did Melvyn Bragg first
present 'The South Bank Show' on ITV?

A: 1970

B: 1974

C: 1978

D: 1982

20

Commonwealth Day is celebrated on
the second Monday of which month?

A: March

B: April

C: May

D: June

If you would like to use your 50:50 please turn to page 254
If you would like to Ask The Audience please turn to page 267
Turn to the answer section on page 274 to find out if you've won £500,000!

21

With which philosopher do you associate the quotation 'Cogito ergo sum' - 'I think therefore I am'?

- A: Socrates
- B: Rousseau
- C: Aristotle
- D: Descartes

22

Which Moscow building was the headquarters of the Parliament of the Russian Republic?

- A: The White House
- B: The Red Citadel
- C: The Winter Palace
- D: The Dome

23

In the human body, which protein forms nails and hair?

- A: Keratin
- B: Melanin
- C: Collagen
- D: Haemoglobin

24

Wykehamists are pupils of which public school?

- A: Wellington School
- B: Winchester College
- C: Whitgift School
- D: Wells Cathedral School

25

Which Oxford college was founded in 1899 to provide education specifically for working people?

- A: Wadham
- B: Ruskin
- C: New
- D: Nuffield

If you would like to use your 50:50 please turn to page 254
If you would like to Ask The Audience please turn to page 267
Turn to the answer section on page 274 to find out if you've won £500,000!

26

What was named after Ada, the daughter of the poet Lord Byron?

A: Oxford college

B: Computer language

C: Firework

D: Spaniel

27

In medieval legend, who was the lover of Isolde?

A: Abelard

B: Siegfried

C: Tristan

D: Roland

28

Selene was the Greek goddess of what?

A: Sun

B: Moon

C: Rainbow

D: Youth

29

In which month in 1952 did the Queen accede to the throne?

A: January

B: February

C: March

D: April

30

Who played Hopalong Cassidy in the 1950s TV series?

A: Fess Parker

B: William Boyd

C: Alan Hale Jr.

D: Clayton Moore

If you would like to use your 50:50 please turn to page 254
If you would like to Ask The Audience please turn to page 267
Turn to the answer section on page 274 to find out if you've won £500,000!

31

In which Dickens novel does Dr Slammer appear?

A: Dombey and Son
B: The Pickwick Papers
C: David Copperfield
D: Little Dorrit

32

According to the Bible, what did God create on the third day?

A: Land and sea
B: Day and night
C: Man
D: Sun and moon

33

Which of these countries has virtually the same size population as the UK?

A: Spain
B: France
C: Germany
D: Romania

34

As what is Carol Ann Duffy best known?

A: Architect
B: Poet
C: Opera singer
D: Golfer

35

On which Hawaiian island is Waikiki Beach?

A: Hawaii
B: Maui
C: Oahu
D: Kauai

If you would like to use your 50:50 please turn to page 254
If you would like to Ask The Audience please turn to page 267
Turn to the answer section on page 274 to find out if you've won £500,000!

36

In which century was the artist Michelangelo born?

A: 13th

B: 14th

C: 15th

D: 16th

If you would like to use your 50:50 please turn to page 254
If you would like to Ask The Audience please turn to page 267
Turn to the answer section on page 274 to find out if you've won £500,000!

15	◆	**£1 MILLION**
14	◆	£500,000
13	◆	£250,000
12	◆	£125,000
11	◆	£64,000
10	◆	£32,000
9	◆	£16,000
8	◆	£8,000
7	◆	£4,000
6	◆	£2,000
5	◆	£1,000
4	◆	£500
3	◆	£300
2	◆	£200
1	◆	£100

15 ♦ £1,000,000

1

Which popular garden flower has a name that means 'water vessel' in Greek?

- A: Aquilegia
- B: Hydrangea
- C: Antirrhinum
- D: Hibiscus

2

Which of Henry VIII's wives was the widow of his elder brother Arthur?

- A: Catherine of Aragon
- B: Anne of Cleves
- C: Catherine Howard
- D: Catherine Parr

3

What are you afraid of if you suffer from ailurophobia?

- A: Bats
- B: Cats
- C: Rats
- D: Gnats

4

Which people are specifically excluded from inheritance and succession in Salic Law?

- A: Children under 15
- B: Women
- C: Divorcees
- D: Illegitimate children

5

'The Boys from Syracuse' is a musical based on which Shakespeare play?

- A: The Comedy of Errors
- B: As You Like It
- C: Twelfth Night
- D: The Tempest

If you would like to use your 50:50 please turn to page 254
If you would like to Ask The Audience please turn to page 268
Turn to the answer section on page 274 to find out if you've won £1,000,000!

6

Wattle is the national emblem of which country?

- A: Australia
- B: Kenya
- C: Mexico
- D: Argentina

7

What is the chief ore of mercury?

- A: Galena
- B: Cinnabar
- C: Siderite
- D: Malachite

8

Edward Whymper was the first man to climb which of these mountains?

- A: Matterhorn
- B: K2
- C: Olympus
- D: Eiger

9

Cheyenne is the capital of which American state?

- A: Nebraska
- B: Wyoming
- C: Kansas
- D: Utah

10

Guru Nanak was the founder of which religion?

- A: Hinduism
- B: Islam
- C: Sikhism
- D: Buddhism

If you would like to use your 50:50 please turn to page 254
If you would like to Ask The Audience please turn to page 268
Turn to the answer section on page 274 to find out if you've won £1,000,000!

11

Gules is the heraldic name for which colour?

A: Red
B: Blue
C: Silver
D: Black

12

In which mythology was Hathor the goddess of the sky?

A: Egyptian
B: Roman
C: Celtic
D: Norse

13

What was the first name of L. Frank Baum, author of 'The Wonderful Wizard of Oz'?

A: Linus
B: Lyman
C: Lionel
D: Leon

14

Which famous battle was fought on St Crispin's Day?

A: Agincourt
B: Waterloo
C: Trafalgar
D: Balaclava

15

What name is given to the larva of a click beetle?

A: Leatherjacket
B: Silverfish
C: Wireworm
D: Spanish fly

If you would like to use your 50:50 please turn to page 254
If you would like to Ask The Audience please turn to page 268
Turn to the answer section on page 274 to find out if you've won £1,000,000!

16

In which year was Mahatma Gandhi assassinated?

- A: 1946
- B: 1947
- C: 1948
- D: 1949

17

What is the name of the largest moon of Jupiter?

- A: Io
- B: Europa
- C: Ganymede
- D: Callisto

18

What is a 'clerihew'?

- A: Limestone block
- B: Covered walkway
- C: Humorous verse
- D: Genetic replica

19

John Stafford Smith composed the tune of which national anthem?

- A: Advance Australia Fair
- B: O Canada
- C: The Star-Spangled Banner
- D: God Save the Queen

20

In Greek mythology, Gaia was the goddess of what?

- A: Sky
- B: Wind
- C: Sea
- D: Earth

If you would like to use your 50:50 please turn to page 254
If you would like to Ask The Audience please turn to page 268
Turn to the answer section on page 274 to find out if you've won £1,000,000!

21

In which country is the port of Fray Bentos?

A: Argentina
B: Paraguay
C: Uruguay
D: Chile

22

Which word means a tapering piece of material used in making a skirt or umbrella?

A: Murphy
B: Gore
C: Faulkner
D: Pollitt

23

Which country's international car registration is T?

A: Turkey
B: Tunisia
C: Togo
D: Thailand

24

Which football team won the FA Cup in 1927?

A: Aston Villa
B: Burnley
C: Cardiff City
D: Derby County

25

Which of these wine bottles is about six times the standard size?

A: Methuselah
B: Rehoboam
C: Salmanazar
D: Balthazar

If you would like to use your 50:50 please turn to page 254
If you would like to Ask The Audience please turn to page 268
Turn to the answer section on page 274 to find out if you've won £1,000,000!

26

Which of these countries is the largest in area?

A: Republic of Ireland
B: Hungary
C: Iceland
D: Austria

27

Which was the first college at Cambridge University?

A: Christ's
B: Peterhouse
C: Trinity
D: Jesus

28

Katja Seizinger is associated with which sport?

A: Gymnastics
B: Badminton
C: Skiing
D: Swimming

29

Red, white and which other colour appear on the Hungarian flag?

A: Blue
B: Black
C: Yellow
D: Green

30

Who was the mother of Charles I?

A: Caroline of Ansbach
B: Anne of Denmark
C: Isabella of France
D: Mary of Modena

If you would like to use your 50:50 please turn to page 254
If you would like to Ask The Audience please turn to page 268
Turn to the answer section on page 274 to find out if you've won £1,000,000!

15 ◆ £1,000,000

31

Dubris was the Roman name for which town?

A: Darlington

B: Doncaster

C: Dover

D: Durham

32

In mythology, who was the husband of Eurydice?

A: Daphnis

B: Narcissus

C: Orpheus

D: Pan

If you would like to use your 50:50 please turn to page 254
If you would like to Ask The Audience please turn to page 268
Turn to the answer section on page 274 to find out if you've won £1,000,000!

50:50

£100

1	options remaining are B and C	38	options remaining are B and C
2	options remaining are B and C	39	options remaining are A and B
3	options remaining are A and D	40	options remaining are C and D
4	options remaining are A and C	41	options remaining are A and B
5	options remaining are B and D	42	options remaining are B and C
6	options remaining are A and B	43	options remaining are A and C
7	options remaining are B and C	44	options remaining are B and D
8	options remaining are B and D	45	options remaining are A and C
9	options remaining are A and B	46	options remaining are A and B
10	options remaining are A and D	47	options remaining are B and C
11	options remaining are B and D	48	options remaining are B and C
12	options remaining are B and C	49	options remaining are B and C
13	options remaining are B and C	50	options remaining are B and C
14	options remaining are A and C	51	options remaining are A and B
15	options remaining are A and B	52	options remaining are B and C
16	options remaining are B and C	53	options remaining are A and D
17	options remaining are A and B	54	options remaining are A and B
18	options remaining are B and C	55	options remaining are B and C
19	options remaining are B and C	56	options remaining are B and C
20	options remaining are A and D	57	options remaining are B and D
21	options remaining are A and B	58	options remaining are A and C
22	options remaining are B and D	59	options remaining are A and B
23	options remaining are B and C	60	options remaining are A and B
24	options remaining are A and C	61	options remaining are A and B
25	options remaining are C and D	62	options remaining are A and B
26	options remaining are A and B	63	options remaining are A and B
27	options remaining are C and D	64	options remaining are A and B
28	options remaining are A and C	65	options remaining are B and D
29	options remaining are A and C	66	options remaining are B and C
30	options remaining are A and C	67	options remaining are A and D
31	options remaining are A and C	68	options remaining are B and C
32	options remaining are A and B	69	options remaining are A and C
33	options remaining are A and C	70	options remaining are C and D
34	options remaining are B and C	71	options remaining are A and C
35	options remaining are B and C	72	options remaining are A and B
36	options remaining are C and D	73	options remaining are B and C
37	options remaining are B and D	74	options remaining are B and D

50:50

75 options remaining are A and B
76 options remaining are B and C
77 options remaining are B and D
78 options remaining are A and B
79 options remaining are A and C
80 options remaining are B and D
81 options remaining are C and D
82 options remaining are A and D
83 options remaining are B and C
84 options remaining are A and C
85 options remaining are A and B
86 options remaining are A and B
87 options remaining are A and B
88 options remaining are A and C

£200

1 options remaining are A and C
2 options remaining are C and D
3 options remaining are B and C
4 options remaining are A and D
5 options remaining are B and C
6 options remaining are B and D
7 options remaining are A and C
8 options remaining are B and C
9 options remaining are A and C
10 options remaining are A and B
11 options remaining are A and C
12 options remaining are B and C
13 options remaining are A and C
14 options remaining are B and D
15 options remaining are C and D
16 options remaining are B and C
17 options remaining are B and C
18 options remaining are C and D
19 options remaining are C and D
20 options remaining are A and B
21 options remaining are A and B
22 options remaining are C and D
23 options remaining are A and C
24 options remaining are A and C
25 options remaining are B and C
26 options remaining are B and D
27 options remaining are A and C
28 options remaining are C and D
29 options remaining are A and D
30 options remaining are A and C
31 options remaining are A and D
32 options remaining are A and B
33 options remaining are B and C
34 options remaining are A and B
35 options remaining are A and B
36 options remaining are B and D
37 options remaining are A and B
38 options remaining are C and D
39 options remaining are A and C
40 options remaining are A and B
41 options remaining are A and D
42 options remaining are B and C

50:50

£300

43	options remaining are B and C	1	options remaining are B and D
44	options remaining are B and C	2	options remaining are C and D
45	options remaining are B and D	3	options remaining are B and C
46	options remaining are C and D	4	options remaining are B and D
47	options remaining are B and C	5	options remaining are C and D
48	options remaining are A and B	6	options remaining are C and D
49	options remaining are A and C	7	options remaining are B and C
50	options remaining are A and B	8	options remaining are A and C
51	options remaining are A and B	9	options remaining are B and D
52	options remaining are A and B	10	options remaining are A and B
53	options remaining are B and C	11	options remaining are B and C
54	options remaining are B and D	12	options remaining are A and C
55	options remaining are B and D	13	options remaining are A and C
56	options remaining are C and D	14	options remaining are A and C
57	options remaining are A and B	15	options remaining are A and D
58	options remaining are A and B	16	options remaining are B and D
59	options remaining are C and D	17	options remaining are C and D
60	options remaining are B and C	18	options remaining are B and C
61	options remaining are C and D	19	options remaining are A and B
62	options remaining are B and C	20	options remaining are A and B
63	options remaining are C and D	21	options remaining are C and D
64	options remaining are A and B	22	options remaining are B and D
65	options remaining are C and D	23	options remaining are A and C
66	options remaining are A and B	24	options remaining are C and D
67	options remaining are B and D	25	options remaining are B and C
68	options remaining are A and B	26	options remaining are A and C
69	options remaining are A and D	27	options remaining are B and D
70	options remaining are B and D	28	options remaining are A and B
71	options remaining are C and D	29	options remaining are C and D
72	options remaining are A and D	30	options remaining are B and C
73	options remaining are A and B	31	options remaining are A and C
74	options remaining are A and D	32	options remaining are B and D
75	options remaining are B and C	33	options remaining are C and D
76	options remaining are C and D	34	options remaining are A and D
77	options remaining are A and C	35	options remaining are B and D
78	options remaining are B and D	36	options remaining are A and B
79	options remaining are A and B	37	options remaining are B and C
80	options remaining are B and C	38	options remaining are B and D
81	options remaining are C and D	39	options remaining are C and D
82	options remaining are A and C	40	options remaining are C and D
83	options remaining are A and B	41	options remaining are A and D
84	options remaining are A and C	42	options remaining are A and D

50:50

£500

43	options remaining are A and C	1	options remaining are B and D
44	options remaining are A and C	2	options remaining are A and C
45	options remaining are B and C	3	options remaining are B and C
46	options remaining are A and B	4	options remaining are A and B
47	options remaining are C and D	5	options remaining are A and B
48	options remaining are C and D	6	options remaining are B and C
49	options remaining are B and C	7	options remaining are A and C
50	options remaining are B and C	8	options remaining are A and C
51	options remaining are C and D	9	options remaining are B and D
52	options remaining are A and B	10	options remaining are A and C
53	options remaining are A and D	11	options remaining are A and B
54	options remaining are B and C	12	options remaining are B and D
55	options remaining are C and D	13	options remaining are A and C
56	options remaining are A and D	14	options remaining are A and C
57	options remaining are B and C	15	options remaining are C and D
58	options remaining are C and D	16	options remaining are A and D
59	options remaining are A and C	17	options remaining are A and D
60	options remaining are B and C	18	options remaining are C and D
61	options remaining are C and D	19	options remaining are B and D
62	options remaining are A and B	20	options remaining are A and C
63	options remaining are A and C	21	options remaining are A and D
64	options remaining are B and D	22	options remaining are C and D
65	options remaining are A and C	23	options remaining are A and D
66	options remaining are A and C	24	options remaining are A and B
67	options remaining are C and D	25	options remaining are B and C
68	options remaining are C and D	26	options remaining are B and D
69	options remaining are A and C	27	options remaining are A and B
70	options remaining are A and B	28	options remaining are B and D
71	options remaining are B and C	29	options remaining are B and C
72	options remaining are B and D	30	options remaining are B and D
73	options remaining are C and D	31	options remaining are A and B
74	options remaining are B and C	32	options remaining are A and C
75	options remaining are B and C	33	options remaining are A and B
76	options remaining are A and C	34	options remaining are A and B
77	options remaining are B and D	35	options remaining are A and C
78	options remaining are A and D	36	options remaining are B and C
79	options remaining are C and D	37	options remaining are A and C
80	options remaining are A and C	38	options remaining are B and C
		39	options remaining are A and C
		40	options remaining are A and B
		41	options remaining are B and C
		42	options remaining are C and D

50:50

£1,000

43 options remaining are B and D	1 options remaining are A and B
44 options remaining are C and D	2 options remaining are B and C
45 options remaining are A and C	3 options remaining are A and C
46 options remaining are A and D	4 options remaining are C and D
47 options remaining are A and D	5 options remaining are C and D
48 options remaining are A and B	6 options remaining are A and B
49 options remaining are A and C	7 options remaining are B and D
50 options remaining are A and B	8 options remaining are A and D
51 options remaining are B and C	9 options remaining are A and C
52 options remaining are A and C	10 options remaining are C and D
53 options remaining are A and D	11 options remaining are A and C
54 options remaining are A and C	12 options remaining are A and B
55 options remaining are A and C	13 options remaining are B and C
56 options remaining are B and C	14 options remaining are A and D
57 options remaining are B and D	15 options remaining are A and C
58 options remaining are A and C	16 options remaining are A and B
59 options remaining are B and D	17 options remaining are A and C
60 options remaining are B and D	18 options remaining are B and C
61 options remaining are C and D	19 options remaining are A and C
62 options remaining are A and B	20 options remaining are A and C
63 options remaining are A and C	21 options remaining are B and D
64 options remaining are A and C	22 options remaining are C and D
65 options remaining are B and C	23 options remaining are A and D
66 options remaining are B and D	24 options remaining are B and D
67 options remaining are B and C	25 options remaining are B and D
68 options remaining are B and C	26 options remaining are A and B
69 options remaining are A and B	27 options remaining are A and D
70 options remaining are B and D	28 options remaining are B and D
71 options remaining are A and D	29 options remaining are A and D
72 options remaining are A and B	30 options remaining are A and C
73 options remaining are C and D	31 options remaining are A and C
74 options remaining are A and D	32 options remaining are A and B
75 options remaining are A and B	33 options remaining are A and D
76 options remaining are B and C	34 options remaining are C and D
	35 options remaining are B and D
	36 options remaining are B and C
	37 options remaining are C and D
	38 options remaining are B and C
	39 options remaining are B and D
	40 options remaining are A and B
	41 options remaining are B and D
	42 options remaining are C and D

50:50

£2,000

43 options remaining are B and C	1 options remaining are A and D
44 options remaining are A and C	2 options remaining are B and C
45 options remaining are A and B	3 options remaining are A and B
46 options remaining are B and C	4 options remaining are B and C
47 options remaining are B and D	5 options remaining are B and C
48 options remaining are A and C	6 options remaining are A and C
49 options remaining are C and D	7 options remaining are C and D
50 options remaining are A and C	8 options remaining are C and D
51 options remaining are A and C	9 options remaining are A and D
52 options remaining are A and D	10 options remaining are A and D
53 options remaining are A and C	11 options remaining are B and D
54 options remaining are C and D	12 options remaining are C and D
55 options remaining are C and D	13 options remaining are A and C
56 options remaining are A and C	14 options remaining are C and D
57 options remaining are A and C	15 options remaining are A and D
58 options remaining are A and D	16 options remaining are A and C
59 options remaining are A and B	17 options remaining are A and C
60 options remaining are A and C	18 options remaining are A and D
61 options remaining are B and C	19 options remaining are A and B
62 options remaining are A and D	20 options remaining are A and C
63 options remaining are A and B	21 options remaining are B and D
64 options remaining are B and C	22 options remaining are B and D
65 options remaining are A and C	23 options remaining are C and D
66 options remaining are C and D	24 options remaining are B and D
67 options remaining are B and C	25 options remaining are A and B
68 options remaining are A and C	26 options remaining are B and C
69 options remaining are B and D	27 options remaining are A and C
70 options remaining are B and D	28 options remaining are B and C
71 options remaining are C and D	29 options remaining are B and D
72 options remaining are B and C	30 options remaining are A and C
	31 options remaining are B and C
	32 options remaining are A and B
	33 options remaining are B and D
	34 options remaining are A and C
	35 options remaining are C and D
	36 options remaining are A and D
	37 options remaining are A and B
	38 options remaining are A and D
	39 options remaining are A and C
	40 options remaining are A and C
	41 options remaining are B and D
	42 options remaining are C and D

50:50

43 options remaining are B and D	1 options remaining are B and D
44 options remaining are B and D	2 options remaining are B and D
45 options remaining are A and C	3 options remaining are A and C
46 options remaining are B and C	4 options remaining are A and C
47 options remaining are A and C	5 options remaining are A and C
48 options remaining are A and C	6 options remaining are B and D
49 options remaining are B and D	7 options remaining are B and D
50 options remaining are A and D	8 options remaining are C and D
51 options remaining are A and C	9 options remaining are B and C
52 options remaining are A and C	10 options remaining are B and C
53 options remaining are A and C	11 options remaining are A and D
54 options remaining are A and B	12 options remaining are A and B
55 options remaining are A and C	13 options remaining are A and D
56 options remaining are C and D	14 options remaining are A and C
57 options remaining are B and D	15 options remaining are B and C
58 options remaining are B and D	16 options remaining are A and D
59 options remaining are A and C	17 options remaining are A and B
60 options remaining are A and C	18 options remaining are A and C
61 options remaining are A and C	19 options remaining are A and D
62 options remaining are A and B	20 options remaining are B and C
63 options remaining are A and C	21 options remaining are A and B
64 options remaining are A and B	22 options remaining are C and D
65 options remaining are B and C	23 options remaining are B and C
66 options remaining are A and C	24 options remaining are A and B
67 options remaining are B and C	25 options remaining are A and B
68 options remaining are C and D	26 options remaining are A and D
	27 options remaining are A and D
	28 options remaining are B and C
	29 options remaining are B and C
	30 options remaining are C and D
	31 options remaining are A and C
	32 options remaining are A and C
	33 options remaining are A and C
	34 options remaining are A and B
	35 options remaining are A and D
	36 options remaining are B and C
	37 options remaining are C and D
	38 options remaining are A and B
	39 options remaining are C and D
	40 options remaining are A and C
	41 options remaining are B and D
	42 options remaining are A and D

50:50

£8,000

43 options remaining are B and D		1 options remaining are B and C
44 options remaining are C and D		2 options remaining are C and D
45 options remaining are C and D		3 options remaining are B and D
46 options remaining are A and B		4 options remaining are B and C
47 options remaining are A and B		5 options remaining are A and D
48 options remaining are C and D		6 options remaining are A and D
49 options remaining are B and C		7 options remaining are B and C
50 options remaining are B and C		8 options remaining are A and B
51 options remaining are B and D		9 options remaining are C and D
52 options remaining are C and D		10 options remaining are B and D
53 options remaining are C and D		11 options remaining are A and C
54 options remaining are C and D		12 options remaining are B and D
55 options remaining are B and D		13 options remaining are C and D
56 options remaining are B and D		14 options remaining are A and B
57 options remaining are A and D		15 options remaining are C and D
58 options remaining are A and C		16 options remaining are C and D
59 options remaining are B and D		17 options remaining are B and C
60 options remaining are B and C		18 options remaining are B and C
61 options remaining are A and D		19 options remaining are A and C
62 options remaining are B and C		20 options remaining are B and C
63 options remaining are B and C		21 options remaining are A and B
64 options remaining are B and D		22 options remaining are A and D
		23 options remaining are C and D
		24 options remaining are A and C
		25 options remaining are A and C
		26 options remaining are C and D
		27 options remaining are A and B
		28 options remaining are A and B
		29 options remaining are B and D
		30 options remaining are B and C
		31 options remaining are B and C
		32 options remaining are B and D
		33 options remaining are A and D
		34 options remaining are A and C
		35 options remaining are A and D
		36 options remaining are A and B
		37 options remaining are B and D
		38 options remaining are B and C
		39 options remaining are B and C
		40 options remaining are B and C
		41 options remaining are C and D
		42 options remaining are A and D

50:50

£16,000

43 options remaining are C and D	1 options remaining are C and D
44 options remaining are A and D	2 options remaining are A and C
45 options remaining are C and D	3 options remaining are A and C
46 options remaining are B and D	4 options remaining are A and B
47 options remaining are A and C	5 options remaining are B and C
48 options remaining are B and D	6 options remaining are B and D
49 options remaining are C and D	7 options remaining are A and B
50 options remaining are B and C	8 options remaining are A and D
51 options remaining are A and C	9 options remaining are A and C
52 options remaining are B and C	10 options remaining are B and D
53 options remaining are B and C	11 options remaining are A and C
54 options remaining are C and D	12 options remaining are A and C
55 options remaining are A and C	13 options remaining are A and C
56 options remaining are A and D	14 options remaining are B and C
57 options remaining are B and D	15 options remaining are B and C
58 options remaining are B and D	16 options remaining are C and D
59 options remaining are A and B	17 options remaining are B and D
60 options remaining are B and D	18 options remaining are C and D
	19 options remaining are A and B
	20 options remaining are B and C
	21 options remaining are A and B
	22 options remaining are A and C
	23 options remaining are B and C
	24 options remaining are B and C
	25 options remaining are A and D
	26 options remaining are A and C
	27 options remaining are B and D
	28 options remaining are B and D
	29 options remaining are B and C
	30 options remaining are A and B
	31 options remaining are A and B
	32 options remaining are A and C
	33 options remaining are A and C
	34 options remaining are B and C
	35 options remaining are C and D
	36 options remaining are B and C
	37 options remaining are A and B
	38 options remaining are B and C
	39 options remaining are A and B
	40 options remaining are A and D
	41 options remaining are A and B
	42 options remaining are B and D

50:50

43	options remaining are A and D
44	options remaining are A and D
45	options remaining are A and D
46	options remaining are C and D
47	options remaining are B and D
48	options remaining are C and D
49	options remaining are C and D
50	options remaining are A and B
51	options remaining are B and C
52	options remaining are A and C
53	options remaining are B and D
54	options remaining are B and C
55	options remaining are B and C
56	options remaining are A and B

1	options remaining are A and D
2	options remaining are A and B
3	options remaining are A and D
4	options remaining are B and C
5	options remaining are A and C
6	options remaining are B and D
7	options remaining are A and B
8	options remaining are C and D
9	options remaining are C and D
10	options remaining are A and B
11	options remaining are B and D
12	options remaining are C and D
13	options remaining are B and C
14	options remaining are B and C
15	options remaining are A and D
16	options remaining are B and C
17	options remaining are A and D
18	options remaining are A and B
19	options remaining are A and B
20	options remaining are B and D
21	options remaining are A and B
22	options remaining are C and D
23	options remaining are C and D
24	options remaining are A and D
25	options remaining are A and B
26	options remaining are A and B
27	options remaining are A and B
28	options remaining are A and B
29	options remaining are A and B
30	options remaining are A and B
31	options remaining are A and B
32	options remaining are A and B
33	options remaining are A and C
34	options remaining are B and C
35	options remaining are A and C
36	options remaining are A and D
37	options remaining are B and D
38	options remaining are A and C
39	options remaining are B and D
40	options remaining are A and C
41	options remaining are A and D
42	options remaining are A and B

50:50

£64,000

43 options remaining are B and D	1 options remaining are A and B
44 options remaining are B and D	2 options remaining are C and D
45 options remaining are A and B	3 options remaining are B and C
46 options remaining are A and C	4 options remaining are C and D
47 options remaining are C and D	5 options remaining are A and B
48 options remaining are A and B	6 options remaining are A and C
49 options remaining are C and D	7 options remaining are B and C
50 options remaining are B and D	8 options remaining are A and B
51 options remaining are A and B	9 options remaining are B and C
52 options remaining are A and C	10 options remaining are A and B
	11 options remaining are A and D
	12 options remaining are A and D
	13 options remaining are A and B
	14 options remaining are A and D
	15 options remaining are A and B
	16 options remaining are C and D
	17 options remaining are A and C
	18 options remaining are A and D
	19 options remaining are A and D
	20 options remaining are A and B
	21 options remaining are A and B
	22 options remaining are A and D
	23 options remaining are A and D
	24 options remaining are B and C
	25 options remaining are B and D
	26 options remaining are C and D
	27 options remaining are A and C
	28 options remaining are B and D
	29 options remaining are C and D
	30 options remaining are A and C
	31 options remaining are B and D
	32 options remaining are B and C
	33 options remaining are A and B
	34 options remaining are B and D
	35 options remaining are A and D
	36 options remaining are A and B
	37 options remaining are A and D
	38 options remaining are A and B
	39 options remaining are B and C
	40 options remaining are B and D
	41 options remaining are C and D
	42 options remaining are A and B

50:50

£125,000

43 options remaining are A and C
44 options remaining are A and D
45 options remaining are A and B
46 options remaining are C and D
47 options remaining are B and D
48 options remaining are B and C

1 options remaining are C and D
2 options remaining are A and B
3 options remaining are A and B
4 options remaining are B and D
5 options remaining are A and C
6 options remaining are C and D
7 options remaining are A and C
8 options remaining are A and B
9 options remaining are A and B
10 options remaining are B and C
11 options remaining are A and B
12 options remaining are B and C
13 options remaining are B and C
14 options remaining are B and D
15 options remaining are A and B
16 options remaining are B and C
17 options remaining are A and C
18 options remaining are A and D
19 options remaining are C and D
20 options remaining are A and D
21 options remaining are A and D
22 options remaining are A and D
23 options remaining are A and B
24 options remaining are B and C
25 options remaining are B and C
26 options remaining are A and C
27 options remaining are A and D
28 options remaining are C and D
29 options remaining are A and C
30 options remaining are A and B
31 options remaining are A and B
32 options remaining are A and D
33 options remaining are C and D
34 options remaining are A and C
35 options remaining are A and D
36 options remaining are A and D
37 options remaining are B and C
38 options remaining are B and C
39 options remaining are A and B
40 options remaining are B and C
41 options remaining are A and D
42 options remaining are A and B

50:50

43 options remaining are A and D
44 options remaining are B and D

£250,000

1   options remaining are A and B
2   options remaining are A and D
3   options remaining are A and C
4   options remaining are B and D
5   options remaining are B and D
6   options remaining are C and D
7   options remaining are A and B
8   options remaining are A and D
9   options remaining are B and D
10 options remaining are C and D
11 options remaining are B and D
12 options remaining are B and C
13 options remaining are A and B
14 options remaining are B and C
15 options remaining are A and D
16 options remaining are A and B
17 options remaining are A and D
18 options remaining are B and D
19 options remaining are A and B
20 options remaining are A and D
21 options remaining are A and B
22 options remaining are B and D
23 options remaining are B and D
24 options remaining are C and D
25 options remaining are C and D
26 options remaining are C and D
27 options remaining are A and B
28 options remaining are A and B
29 options remaining are B and C
30 options remaining are A and C
31 options remaining are B and D
32 options remaining are A and C
33 options remaining are B and C
34 options remaining are C and D
35 options remaining are A and C
36 options remaining are B and D
37 options remaining are C and D
38 options remaining are B and C
39 options remaining are C and D
40 options remaining are B and C

50:50

£500,000

1 options remaining are C and D
2 options remaining are B and C
3 options remaining are A and B
4 options remaining are A and D
5 options remaining are C and D
6 options remaining are A and D
7 options remaining are A and B
8 options remaining are B and D
9 options remaining are A and D
10 options remaining are A and D
11 options remaining are B and D
12 options remaining are A and C
13 options remaining are B and C
14 options remaining are B and D
15 options remaining are C and D
16 options remaining are C and D
17 options remaining are B and C
18 options remaining are B and C
19 options remaining are B and C
20 options remaining are A and C
21 options remaining are B and D
22 options remaining are A and C
23 options remaining are A and C
24 options remaining are A and B
25 options remaining are B and C
26 options remaining are A and B
27 options remaining are C and D
28 options remaining are A and B
29 options remaining are A and B
30 options remaining are B and C
31 options remaining are A and B
32 options remaining are A and B
33 options remaining are A and B
34 options remaining are B and C
35 options remaining are B and C
36 options remaining are C and D

£1,000,000

1 options remaining are A and B
2 options remaining are A and B
3 options remaining are B and C
4 options remaining are A and B
5 options remaining are A and D
6 options remaining are A and D
7 options remaining are A and B
8 options remaining are A and B
9 options remaining are A and B
10 options remaining are A and C
11 options remaining are A and B
12 options remaining are A and C
13 options remaining are A and B
14 options remaining are A and B
15 options remaining are A and C
16 options remaining are B and C
17 options remaining are B and C
18 options remaining are B and C
19 options remaining are B and C
20 options remaining are A and D
21 options remaining are B and C
22 options remaining are B and D
23 options remaining are A and D
24 options remaining are B and C
25 options remaining are A and B
26 options remaining are B and C
27 options remaining are B and C
28 options remaining are C and D
29 options remaining are A and D
30 options remaining are B and C
31 options remaining are C and D
32 options remaining are B and C

Ask the Audience

£100

1	A: 2%	B: 98%	C: 0%	D: 0%
2	A: 0%	B: 0%	C: 100%	D: 0%
3	A: 0%	B: 0%	C: 1%	D: 99%
4	A: 0%	B: 0%	C: 100%	D: 0%
5	A: 1%	B: 0%	C: 0%	D: 99%
6	A: 2%	B: 95%	C: 3%	D: 0%
7	A: 0%	B: 100%	C: 0%	D: 0%
8	A: 0%	B: 100%	C: 0%	D: 0%
9	A: 100%	B: 0%	C: 0%	D: 0%
10	A: 100%	B: 0%	C: 0%	D: 0%
11	A: 0%	B: 1%	C: 0%	D: 99%
12	A: 0%	B: 100%	C: 0%	D: 0%
13	A: 27%	B: 53%	C: 9%	D: 11%
14	A: 0%	B: 0%	C: 100%	D: 0%
15	A: 100%	B: 0%	C: 0%	D: 0%
16	A: 0%	B: 0%	C: 100%	D: 0%
17	A: 98%	B: 2%	C: 0%	D: 0%
18	A: 0%	B: 0%	C: 100%	D: 0%
19	A: 0%	B: 99%	C: 1%	D: 0%
20	A: 0%	B: 0%	C: 3%	D: 97%
21	A: 100%	B: 0%	C: 0%	D: 0%
22	A: 0%	B: 0%	C: 0%	D: 100%
23	A: 1%	B: 0%	C: 99%	D: 0%
24	A: 98%	B: 2%	C: 0%	D: 0%
25	A: 0%	B: 0%	C: 3%	D: 97%
26	A: 0%	B: 100%	C: 0%	D: 0%
27	A: 0%	B: 0%	C: 96%	D: 4%
28	A: 0%	B: 0%	C: 100%	D: 0%
29	A: 81%	B: 4%	C: 15%	D: 0%
30	A: 0%	B: 0%	C: 100%	D: 0%
31	A: 100%	B: 0%	C: 0%	D: 0%
32	A: 2%	B: 98%	C: 0%	D: 0%
33	A: 99%	B: 0%	C: 0%	D: 1%
34	A: 0%	B: 100%	C: 0%	D: 0%
35	A: 0%	B: 0%	C: 100%	D: 0%
36	A: 0%	B: 2%	C: 0%	D: 98%
37	A: 0%	B: 100%	C: 0%	D: 0%
38	A: 0%	B: 100%	C: 0%	D: 0%
39	A: 0%	B: 100%	C: 0%	D: 0%
40	A: 0%	B: 1%	C: 0%	D: 99%
41	A: 0%	B: 100%	C: 0%	D: 0%
42	A: 0%	B: 100%	C: 0%	D: 0%
43	A: 99%	B: 0%	C: 0%	D: 1%
44	A: 0%	B: 100%	C: 0%	D: 0%
45	A: 100%	B: 0%	C: 0%	D: 0%
46	A: 100%	B: 0%	C: 0%	D: 0%
47	A: 0%	B: 100%	C: 0%	D: 0%
48	A: 0%	B: 0%	C: 100%	D: 0%
49	A: 2%	B: 3%	C: 95%	D: 0%
50	A: 0%	B: 100%	C: 0%	D: 0%
51	A: 98%	B: 0%	C: 0%	D: 2%
52	A: 0%	B: 100%	C: 0%	D: 0%
53	A: 99%	B: 0%	C: 0%	D: 1%
54	A: 0%	B: 100%	C: 0%	D: 0%
55	A: 0%	B: 97%	C: 3%	D: 0%
56	A: 0%	B: 0%	C: 100%	D: 0%
57	A: 0%	B: 97%	C: 0%	D: 3%
58	A: 1%	B: 0%	C: 99%	D: 0%
59	A: 100%	B: 0%	C: 0%	D: 0%
60	A: 2%	B: 0%	C: 98%	D: 0%
61	A: 100%	B: 0%	C: 0%	D: 0%
62	A: 0%	B: 100%	C: 0%	D: 0%
63	A: 0%	B: 100%	C: 0%	D: 0%
64	A: 100%	B: 0%	C: 0%	D: 0%
65	A: 0%	B: 100%	C: 0%	D: 0%
66	A: 0%	B: 0%	C: 100%	D: 0%
67	A: 100%	B: 0%	C: 0%	D: 0%
68	A: 5%	B: 91%	C: 0%	D: 4%
69	A: 100%	B: 0%	C: 0%	D: 0%
70	A: 0%	B: 0%	C: 100%	D: 0%
71	A: 100%	B: 0%	C: 0%	D: 0%
72	A: 0%	B: 100%	C: 0%	D: 0%
73	A: 25%	B: 9%	C: 66%	D: 0%
74	A: 0%	B: 100%	C: 0%	D: 0%

ASK THE AUDIENCE

75	A: 0%	B: 100%	C: 0%	D: 0%
76	A: 1%	B: 0%	C: 99%	D: 0%
77	A: 0%	B: 100%	C: 0%	D: 0%
78	A: 100%	B: 0%	C: 0%	D: 0%
79	A: 0%	B: 0%	C: 100%	D: 0%
80	A: 0%	B: 0%	C: 0%	D: 100%
81	A: 0%	B: 0%	C: 100%	D: 0%

82	A: 100%	B: 0%	C: 0%	D: 0%
83	A: 0%	B: 100%	C: 0%	D: 0%
84	A: 100%	B: 0%	C: 0%	D: 0%
85	A: 98%	B: 0%	C: 2%	D: 0%
86	A: 0%	B: 99%	C: 0%	D: 1%
87	A: 100%	B: 0%	C: 0%	D: 0%
88	A: 100%	B: 0%	C: 0%	D: 0%

£200

1	A: 100%	B: 0%	C: 0%	D: 0%
2	A: 0%	B: 0%	C: 100%	D: 0%
3	A: 4%	B: 0%	C: 96%	D: 0%
4	A: 100%	B: 0%	C: 0%	D: 0%
5	A: 0%	B: 0%	C: 100%	D: 0%
6	A: 0%	B: 0%	C: 0%	D: 100%
7	A: 100%	B: 0%	C: 0%	D: 0%
8	A: 0%	B: 0%	C: 100%	D: 0%
9	A: 0%	B: 0%	C: 100%	D: 0%
10	A: 0%	B: 97%	C: 0%	D: 3%
11	A: 0%	B: 22%	C: 78%	D: 0%
12	A: 0%	B: 0%	C: 100%	D: 0%
13	A: 100%	B: 0%	C: 0%	D: 0%
14	A: 0%	B: 0%	C: 0%	D: 100%
15	A: 0%	B: 0%	C: 100%	D: 0%
16	A: 0%	B: 100%	C: 0%	D: 0%
17	A: 9%	B: 0%	C: 91%	D: 0%
18	A: 0%	B: 16%	C: 84%	D: 0%
19	A: 0%	B: 0%	C: 100%	D: 0%
20	A: 0%	B: 100%	C: 0%	D: 0%
21	A: 0%	B: 100%	C: 0%	D: 0%
22	A: 0%	B: 0%	C: 100%	D: 0%
23	A: 0%	B: 0%	C: 100%	D: 0%
24	A: 89%	B: 0%	C: 11%	D: 0%
25	A: 8%	B: 92%	C: 0%	D: 0%
26	A: 0%	B: 100%	C: 0%	D: 0%
27	A: 0%	B: 0%	C: 100%	D: 0%
28	A: 0%	B: 0%	C: 100%	D: 0%
29	A: 100%	B: 0%	C: 0%	D: 0%
30	A: 2%	B: 0%	C: 98%	D: 0%
31	A: 6%	B: 0%	C: 0%	D: 94%
32	A: 0%	B: 100%	C: 0%	D: 0%

33	A: 4%	B: 8%	C: 71%	D: 17%
34	A: 5%	B: 95%	C: 0%	D: 0%
35	A: 3%	B: 0%	C: 97%	D: 0%
36	A: 8%	B: 0%	C: 0%	D: 92%
37	A: 100%	B: 0%	C: 0%	D: 0%
38	A: 4%	B: 0%	C: 0%	D: 96%
39	A: 0%	B: 0%	C: 93%	D: 7%
40	A: 1%	B: 99%	C: 0%	D: 0%
41	A: 100%	B: 0%	C: 0%	D: 0%
42	A: 0%	B: 0%	C: 100%	D: 0%
43	A: 5%	B: 95%	C: 0%	D: 0%
44	A: 0%	B: 100%	C: 0%	D: 0%
45	A: 0%	B: 0%	C: 0%	D: 100%
46	A: 0%	B: 0%	C: 100%	D: 0%
47	A: 0%	B: 100%	C: 0%	D: 0%
48	A: 0%	B: 100%	C: 0%	D: 0%
49	A: 0%	B: 0%	C: 100%	D: 0%
50	A: 99%	B: 0%	C: 0%	D: 1%
51	A: 0%	B: 100%	C: 0%	D: 0%
52	A: 0%	B: 100%	C: 0%	D: 0%
53	A: 0%	B: 100%	C: 0%	D: 0%
54	A: 13%	B: 0%	C: 4%	D: 83%
55	A: 0%	B: 0%	C: 0%	D: 100%
56	A: 0%	B: 0%	C: 9%	D: 91%
57	A: 3%	B: 97%	C: 0%	D: 0%
58	A: 86%	B: 14%	C: 0%	D: 0%
59	A: 0%	B: 0%	C: 100%	D: 0%
60	A: 0%	B: 100%	C: 0%	D: 0%
61	A: 0%	B: 0%	C: 95%	D: 5%
62	A: 0%	B: 0%	C: 100%	D: 0%
63	A: 0%	B: 0%	C: 0%	D: 100%
64	A: 69%	B: 25%	C: 3%	D: 3%

ASK THE AUDIENCE

65	A: 13%	B: 0%	C: 79%	D: 8%	75	A: 0%	B: 7%	C: 93%	D: 0%
66	A: 100%	B: 0%	C: 0%	D: 0%	76	A: 0%	B: 0%	C: 0%	D: 100%
67	A: 3%	B: 0%	C: 0%	D: 97%	77	A: 0%	B: 0%	C: 100%	D: 0%
68	A: 100%	B: 0%	C: 0%	D: 0%	78	A: 0%	B: 100%	C: 0%	D: 0%
69	A: 2%	B: 0%	C: 10%	D: 88%	79	A: 90%	B: 5%	C: 5%	D: 0%
70	A: 0%	B: 100%	C: 0%	D: 0%	80	A: 0%	B: 0%	C: 100%	D: 0%
71	A: 0%	B: 0%	C: 95%	D: 5%	81	A: 0%	B: 0%	C: 3%	D: 97%
72	A: 0%	B: 0%	C: 4%	D: 96%	82	A: 94%	B: 0%	C: 6%	D: 0%
73	A: 0%	B: 100%	C: 0%	D: 0%	83	A: 13%	B: 75%	C: 0%	D: 12%
74	A: 100%	B: 0%	C: 0%	D: 0%	84	A: 14%	B: 0%	C: 86%	D: 0%

£300

1	A: 0%	B: 6%	C: 0%	D: 94%	30	A: 11%	B: 0%	C: 87%	D: 2%
2	A: 0%	B: 0%	C: 7%	D: 93%	31	A: 99%	B: 0%	C: 1%	D: 0%
3	A: 0%	B: 0%	C: 100%	D: 0%	32	A: 0%	B: 0%	C: 0%	D: 100%
4	A: 0%	B: 100%	C: 0%	D: 0%	33	A: 0%	B: 0%	C: 0%	D: 100%
5	A: 27%	B: 5%	C: 7%	D: 61%	34	A: 99%	B: 0%	C: 1%	D: 0%
6	A: 0%	B: 11%	C: 0%	D: 89%	35	A: 0%	B: 100%	C: 0%	D: 0%
7	A: 0%	B: 0%	C: 100%	D: 0%	36	A: 0%	B: 88%	C: 9%	D: 3%
8	A: 11%	B: 0%	C: 83%	D: 6%	37	A: 11%	B: 67%	C: 17%	D: 5%
9	A: 3%	B: 19%	C: 0%	D: 78%	38	A: 0%	B: 0%	C: 0%	D: 100%
10	A: 0%	B: 100%	C: 0%	D: 0%	39	A: 0%	B: 0%	C: 97%	D: 3%
11	A: 2%	B: 0%	C: 98%	D: 0%	40	A: 0%	B: 8%	C: 86%	D: 6%
12	A: 4%	B: 8%	C: 88%	D: 0%	41	A: 0%	B: 0%	C: 0%	D: 100%
13	A: 0%	B: 0%	C: 100%	D: 0%	42	A: 2%	B: 0%	C: 1%	D: 97%
14	A: 0%	B: 0%	C: 100%	D: 0%	43	A: 8%	B: 4%	C: 61%	D: 27%
15	A: 97%	B: 0%	C: 3%	D: 0%	44	A: 5%	B: 0%	C: 95%	D: 0%
16	A: 0%	B: 100%	C: 0%	D: 0%	45	A: 6%	B: 89%	C: 0%	D: 5%
17	A: 0%	B: 0%	C: 0%	D: 100%	46	A: 0%	B: 94%	C: 0%	D: 6%
18	A: 13%	B: 0%	C: 86%	D: 1%	47	A: 0%	B: 0%	C: 93%	D: 7%
19	A: 0%	B: 100%	C: 0%	D: 0%	48	A: 0%	B: 10%	C: 90%	D: 0%
20	A: 0%	B: 100%	C: 0%	D: 0%	49	A: 4%	B: 28%	C: 68%	D: 0%
21	A: 0%	B: 0%	C: 100%	D: 0%	50	A: 0%	B: 0%	C: 100%	D: 0%
22	A: 1%	B: 0%	C: 0%	D: 99%	51	A: 0%	B: 0%	C: 100%	D: 0%
23	A: 100%	B: 0%	C: 0%	D: 0%	52	A: 17%	B: 83%	C: 0%	D: 0%
24	A: 0%	B: 0%	C: 0%	D: 100%	53	A: 0%	B: 0%	C: 44%	D: 56%
25	A: 0%	B: 98%	C: 2%	D: 0%	54	A: 0%	B: 0%	C: 100%	D: 0%
26	A: 15%	B: 0%	C: 85%	D: 0%	55	A: 0%	B: 0%	C: 100%	D: 0%
27	A: 0%	B: 5%	C: 2%	D: 93%	56	A: 98%	B: 0%	C: 0%	D: 2%
28	A: 100%	B: 0%	C: 0%	D: 0%	57	A: 0%	B: 100%	C: 0%	D: 0%
29	A: 0%	B: 0%	C: 0%	D: 100%	58	A: 0%	B: 0%	C: 0%	D: 100%

ASK THE AUDIENCE

59	A: 100%	B: 0%	C: 0%	D: 0%	70	A: 0%	B: 61%	C: 33%	D: 6%
60	A: 0%	B: 0%	C: 100%	D: 0%	71	A: 0%	B: 100%	C: 0%	D: 0%
61	A: 0%	B: 0%	C: 0%	D: 100%	72	A: 15%	B: 0%	C: 0%	D: 85%
62	A: 100%	B: 0%	C: 0%	D: 0%	73	A: 33%	B: 0%	C: 0%	D: 67%
63	A: 0%	B: 0%	C: 100%	D: 0%	74	A: 4%	B: 0%	C: 96%	D: 0%
64	A: 9%	B: 0%	C: 0%	D: 91%	75	A: 0%	B: 0%	C: 100%	D: 0%
65	A: 0%	B: 0%	C: 94%	D: 6%	76	A: 6%	B: 0%	C: 94%	D: 0%
66	A: 22%	B: 0%	C: 78%	D: 0%	77	A: 4%	B: 95%	C: 0%	D: 1%
67	A: 0%	B: 0%	C: 8%	D: 92%	78	A: 98%	B: 0%	C: 0%	D: 2%
68	A: 16%	B: 0%	C: 84%	D: 0%	79	A: 0%	B: 0%	C: 0%	D: 100%
69	A: 0%	B: 0%	C: 100%	D: 0%	80	A: 90%	B: 0%	C: 10%	D: 0%

£500

1	A: 22%	B: 0%	C: 0%	D: 78%	29	A: 0%	B: 0%	C: 100%	D: 0%
2	A: 11%	B: 22%	C: 45%	D: 22%	30	A: 0%	B: 0%	C: 0%	D: 100%
3	A: 0%	B: 1%	C: 99%	D: 0%	31	A: 1%	B: 99%	C: 0%	D: 0%
4	A: 0%	B: 98%	C: 0%	D: 2%	32	A: 72%	B: 0%	C: 25%	D: 3%
5	A: 45%	B: 33%	C: 22%	D: 0%	33	A: 0%	B: 100%	C: 0%	D: 0%
6	A: 0%	B: 0%	C: 100%	D: 0%	34	A: 98%	B: 0%	C: 2%	D: 0%
7	A: 17%	B: 0%	C: 61%	D: 22%	35	A: 17%	B: 11%	C: 61%	D: 11%
8	A: 0%	B: 0%	C: 100%	D: 0%	36	A: 0%	B: 100%	C: 0%	D: 0%
9	A: 0%	B: 0%	C: 0%	D: 100%	37	A: 67%	B: 28%	C: 5%	D: 0%
10	A: 17%	B: 0%	C: 83%	D: 0%	38	A: 0%	B: 0%	C: 100%	D: 0%
11	A: 0%	B: 100%	C: 0%	D: 0%	39	A: 0%	B: 6%	C: 94%	D: 0%
12	A: 4%	B: 0%	C: 0%	D: 96%	40	A: 0%	B: 100%	C: 0%	D: 0%
13	A: 89%	B: 0%	C: 0%	D: 11%	41	A: 0%	B: 0%	C: 100%	D: 0%
14	A: 33%	B: 0%	C: 67%	D: 0%	42	A: 0%	B: 0%	C: 100%	D: 0%
15	A: 0%	B: 0%	C: 100%	D: 0%	43	A: 6%	B: 11%	C: 5%	D: 78%
16	A: 100%	B: 0%	C: 0%	D: 0%	44	A: 0%	B: 0%	C: 0%	D: 100%
17	A: 0%	B: 0%	C: 0%	D: 100%	45	A: 0%	B: 0%	C: 100%	D: 0%
18	A: 0%	B: 0%	C: 100%	D: 0%	46	A: 7%	B: 0%	C: 5%	D: 88%
19	A: 0%	B: 0%	C: 0%	D: 100%	47	A: 99%	B: 1%	C: 0%	D: 0%
20	A: 3%	B: 0%	C: 97%	D: 0%	48	A: 0%	B: 91%	C: 9%	D: 0%
21	A: 100%	B: 0%	C: 0%	D: 0%	49	A: 97%	B: 0%	C: 0%	D: 3%
22	A: 0%	B: 0%	C: 100%	D: 0%	50	A: 83%	B: 0%	C: 0%	D: 17%
23	A: 17%	B: 0%	C: 0%	D: 83%	51	A: 0%	B: 100%	C: 0%	D: 0%
24	A: 0%	B: 100%	C: 0%	D: 0%	52	A: 2%	B: 0%	C: 98%	D: 0%
25	A: 0%	B: 100%	C: 0%	D: 0%	53	A: 82%	B: 0%	C: 7%	D: 11%
26	A: 0%	B: 0%	C: 0%	D: 100%	54	A: 100%	B: 0%	C: 0%	D: 0%
27	A: 78%	B: 13%	C: 9%	D: 0%	55	A: 100%	B: 0%	C: 0%	D: 0%
28	A: 0%	B: 72%	C: 17%	D: 11%	56	A: 5%	B: 61%	C: 16%	D: 18%

57	A: 0%	B: 0%	C: 0%	D: 100%
58	A: 67%	B: 13%	C: 20%	D: 0%
59	A: 0%	B: 100%	C: 0%	D: 0%
60	A: 0%	B: 100%	C: 0%	D: 0%
61	A: 0%	B: 0%	C: 3%	D: 97%
62	A: 12%	B: 83%	C: 0%	D: 5%
63	A: 75%	B: 3%	C: 22%	D: 0%
64	A: 0%	B: 0%	C: 100%	D: 0%
65	A: 15%	B: 0%	C: 85%	D: 0%
66	A: 0%	B: 79%	C: 5%	D: 16%

67	A: 7%	B: 5%	C: 71%	D: 17%
68	A: 0%	B: 84%	C: 10%	D: 6%
69	A: 0%	B: 98%	C: 0%	D: 2%
70	A: 0%	B: 99%	C: 0%	D: 1%
71	A: 92%	B: 0%	C: 0%	D: 8%
72	A: 99%	B: 1%	C: 0%	D: 0%
73	A: 0%	B: 0%	C: 22%	D: 78%
74	A: 0%	B: 0%	C: 0%	D: 100%
75	A: 19%	B: 73%	C: 8%	D: 0%
76	A: 0%	B: 97%	C: 0%	D: 3%

£1,000

1	A: 2%	B: 98%	C: 0%	D: 0%
2	A: 0%	B: 6%	C: 86%	D: 8%
3	A: 3%	B: 0%	C: 97%	D: 0%
4	A: 0%	B: 8%	C: 9%	D: 83%
5	A: 0%	B: 0%	C: 100%	D: 0%
6	A: 52%	B: 48%	C: 0%	D: 0%
7	A: 89%	B: 11%	C: 0%	D: 0%
8	A: 71%	B: 29%	C: 0%	D: 0%
9	A: 31%	B: 12%	C: 57%	D: 0%
10	A: 0%	B: 5%	C: 95%	D: 0%
11	A: 100%	B: 0%	C: 0%	D: 0%
12	A: 21%	B: 79%	C: 0%	D: 0%
13	A: 20%	B: 74%	C: 6%	D: 0%
14	A: 0%	B: 21%	C: 8%	D: 71%
15	A: 29%	B: 8%	C: 54%	D: 9%
16	A: 25%	B: 72%	C: 3%	D: 0%
17	A: 96%	B: 0%	C: 4%	D: 0%
18	A: 17%	B: 0%	C: 72%	D: 11%
19	A: 0%	B: 0%	C: 100%	D: 0%
20	A: 99%	B: 0%	C: 0%	D: 1%
21	A: 21%	B: 43%	C: 0%	D: 36%
22	A: 7%	B: 8%	C: 82%	D: 3%
23	A: 26%	B: 2%	C: 16%	D: 56%
24	A: 5%	B: 73%	C: 9%	D: 13%
25	A: 0%	B: 0%	C: 9%	D: 91%
26	A: 21%	B: 54%	C: 0%	D: 25%
27	A: 0%	B: 2%	C: 0%	D: 98%
28	A: 43%	B: 36%	C: 17%	D: 4%
29	A: 79%	B: 0%	C: 21%	D: 0%

30	A: 97%	B: 3%	C: 0%	D: 0%
31	A: 4%	B: 0%	C: 96%	D: 0%
32	A: 3%	B: 77%	C: 9%	D: 11%
33	A: 64%	B: 0%	C: 5%	D: 31%
34	A: 8%	B: 8%	C: 42%	D: 42%
35	A: 0%	B: 1%	C: 0%	D: 99%
36	A: 0%	B: 21%	C: 79%	D: 0%
37	A: 0%	B: 0%	C: 93%	D: 7%
38	A: 0%	B: 99%	C: 1%	D: 0%
39	A: 6%	B: 16%	C: 6%	D: 72%
40	A: 1%	B: 98%	C: 1%	D: 0%
41	A: 34%	B: 10%	C: 0%	D: 56%
42	A: 0%	B: 1%	C: 99%	D: 0%
43	A: 14%	B: 83%	C: 3%	D: 0%
44	A: 0%	B: 0%	C: 100%	D: 0%
45	A: 43%	B: 21%	C: 0%	D: 36%
46	A: 0%	B: 76%	C: 15%	D: 9%
47	A: 4%	B: 0%	C: 10%	D: 86%
48	A: 1%	B: 0%	C: 99%	D: 0%
49	A: 7%	B: 0%	C: 0%	D: 93%
50	A: 84%	B: 0%	C: 0%	D: 16%
51	A: 0%	B: 4%	C: 96%	D: 0%
52	A: 92%	B: 0%	C: 8%	D: 0%
53	A: 99%	B: 0%	C: 1%	D: 0%
54	A: 11%	B: 15%	C: 11%	D: 63%
55	A: 1%	B: 0%	C: 97%	D: 2%
56	A: 4%	B: 0%	C: 93%	D: 3%
57	A: 4%	B: 0%	C: 84%	D: 12%
58	A: 81%	B: 6%	C: 0%	D: 13%

ASK THE AUDIENCE

59	A: 54%	B: 43%	C: 0%	D: 3%
60	A: 12%	B: 9%	C: 79%	D: 0%
61	A: 9%	B: 91%	C: 0%	D: 0%
62	A: 79%	B: 0%	C: 0%	D: 21%
63	A: 29%	B: 71%	C: 0%	D: 0%
64	A: 16%	B: 12%	C: 72%	D: 0%
65	A: 9%	B: 12%	C: 72%	D: 7%

66	A: 0%	B: 0%	C: 8%	D: 92%
67	A: 5%	B: 83%	C: 12%	D: 0%
68	A: 93%	B: 5%	C: 0%	D: 2%
69	A: 6%	B: 8%	C: 7%	D: 79%
70	A: 35%	B: 55%	C: 10%	D: 0%
71	A: 11%	B: 0%	C: 85%	D: 4%
72	A: 5%	B: 86%	C: 0%	D: 9%

£2,000

1	A: 91%	B: 9%	C: 0%	D: 0%
2	A: 73%	B: 5%	C: 18%	D: 4%
3	A: 64%	B: 9%	C: 21%	D: 6%
4	A: 0%	B: 9%	C: 91%	D: 0%
5	A: 23%	B: 4%	C: 68%	D: 5%
6	A: 15%	B: 0%	C: 71%	D: 14%
7	A: 0%	B: 3%	C: 97%	D: 0%
8	A: 5%	B: 0%	C: 95%	D: 0%
9	A: 92%	B: 0%	C: 8%	D: 0%
10	A: 85%	B: 12%	C: 3%	D: 0%
11	A: 0%	B: 94%	C: 6%	D: 0%
12	A: 4%	B: 5%	C: 14%	D: 77%
13	A: 6%	B: 0%	C: 89%	D: 5%
14	A: 18%	B: 1%	C: 76%	D: 5%
15	A: 91%	B: 2%	C: 7%	D: 0%
16	A: 82%	B: 15%	C: 3%	D: 0%
17	A: 0%	B: 13%	C: 87%	D: 0%
18	A: 81%	B: 4%	C: 10%	D: 5%
19	A: 21%	B: 75%	C: 0%	D: 4%
20	A: 3%	B: 3%	C: 92%	D: 2%
21	A: 0%	B: 99%	C: 0%	D: 1%
22	A: 4%	B: 16%	C: 3%	D: 77%
23	A: 32%	B: 9%	C: 0%	D: 59%
24	A: 11%	B: 0%	C: 0%	D: 89%
25	A: 5%	B: 77%	C: 18%	D: 0%
26	A: 0%	B: 91%	C: 5%	D: 4%
27	A: 2%	B: 15%	C: 83%	D: 0%
28	A: 0%	B: 4%	C: 96%	D: 0%
29	A: 0%	B: 7%	C: 4%	D: 89%
30	A: 9%	B: 0%	C: 91%	D: 0%
31	A: 0%	B: 98%	C: 0%	D: 2%
32	A: 91%	B: 5%	C: 4%	D: 0%

33	A: 15%	B: 3%	C: 0%	D: 82%
34	A: 88%	B: 0%	C: 5%	D: 7%
35	A: 0%	B: 5%	C: 95%	D: 0%
36	A: 99%	B: 1%	C: 0%	D: 0%
37	A: 82%	B: 5%	C: 0%	D: 13%
38	A: 9%	B: 5%	C: 0%	D: 86%
39	A: 2%	B: 0%	C: 98%	D: 0%
40	A: 99%	B: 1%	C: 0%	D: 0%
41	A: 0%	B: 92%	C: 5%	D: 3%
42	A: 18%	B: 9%	C: 0%	D: 73%
43	A: 9%	B: 5%	C: 0%	D: 86%
44	A: 17%	B: 23%	C: 6%	D: 54%
45	A: 5%	B: 4%	C: 91%	D: 0%
46	A: 0%	B: 3%	C: 97%	D: 0%
47	A: 92%	B: 0%	C: 4%	D: 4%
48	A: 89%	B: 1%	C: 3%	D: 7%
49	A: 16%	B: 3%	C: 3%	D: 78%
50	A: 1%	B: 1%	C: 0%	D: 98%
51	A: 5%	B: 0%	C: 86%	D: 9%
52	A: 0%	B: 3%	C: 97%	D: 0%
53	A: 9%	B: 0%	C: 85%	D: 6%
54	A: 77%	B: 18%	C: 0%	D: 5%
55	A: 59%	B: 9%	C: 5%	D: 27%
56	A: 5%	B: 4%	C: 19%	D: 72%
57	A: 0%	B: 94%	C: 0%	D: 6%
58	A: 8%	B: 77%	C: 7%	D: 8%
59	A: 88%	B: 0%	C: 5%	D: 7%
60	A: 0%	B: 0%	C: 95%	D: 5%
61	A: 93%	B: 0%	C: 7%	D: 0%
62	A: 0%	B: 100%	C: 0%	D: 0%
63	A: 2%	B: 0%	C: 97%	D: 1%
64	A: 91%	B: 4%	C: 5%	D: 0%

65 A: 7% B: 0% C: 84% D: 9%
66 A: 36% B: 5% C: 59% D: 0%
67 A: 5% B: 36% C: 41% D: 18%
68 A: 3% B: 14% C: 19% D: 64%

£4,000

1 A: 46% B: 3% C: 44% D: 7%
2 A: 4% B: 55% C: 11% D: 30%
3 A: 10% B: 3% C: 87% D: 0%
4 A: 88% B: 0% C: 7% D: 5%
5 A: 0% B: 0% C: 99% D: 1%
6 A: 0% B: 92% C: 4% D: 4%
7 A: 20% B: 1% C: 3% D: 76%
8 A: 1% B: 0% C: 96% D: 3%
9 A: 0% B: 99% C: 1% D: 0%
10 A: 0% B: 87% C: 11% D: 2%
11 A: 0% B: 3% C: 0% D: 97%
12 A: 92% B: 5% C: 0% D: 3%
13 A: 87% B: 0% C: 0% D: 13%
14 A: 41% B: 17% C: 39% D: 3%
15 A: 3% B: 22% C: 75% D: 0%
16 A: 0% B: 2% C: 0% D: 98%
17 A: 0% B: 96% C: 4% D: 0%
18 A: 63% B: 24% C: 13% D: 0%
19 A: 91% B: 0% C: 9% D: 0%
20 A: 15% B: 52% C: 18% D: 15%
21 A: 47% B: 45% C: 0% D: 8%
22 A: 0% B: 9% C: 91% D: 0%
23 A: 0% B: 98% C: 1% D: 1%
24 A: 10% B: 83% C: 7% D: 0%
25 A: 24% B: 52% C: 0% D: 24%
26 A: 18% B: 7% C: 0% D: 75%
27 A: 9% B: 7% C: 0% D: 84%
28 A: 0% B: 71% C: 24% D: 5%
29 A: 11% B: 77% C: 0% D: 12%
30 A: 0% B: 4% C: 87% D: 9%
31 A: 7% B: 0% C: 93% D: 0%
32 A: 9% B: 15% C: 76% D: 0%
33 A: 99% B: 0% C: 1% D: 0%
34 A: 1% B: 99% C: 0% D: 0%
35 A: 57% B: 15% C: 23% D: 5%
36 A: 18% B: 43% C: 0% D: 39%
37 A: 3% B: 10% C: 35% D: 52%
38 A: 0% B: 98% C: 2% D: 0%
39 A: 31% B: 15% C: 54% D: 0%
40 A: 76% B: 0% C: 19% D: 5%
41 A: 0% B: 83% C: 0% D: 17%
42 A: 0% B: 7% C: 13% D: 80%
43 A: 4% B: 10% C: 0% D: 86%
44 A: 6% B: 7% C: 13% D: 74%
45 A: 0% B: 12% C: 88% D: 0%
46 A: 9% B: 91% C: 0% D: 0%
47 A: 10% B: 79% C: 11% D: 0%
48 A: 12% B: 0% C: 85% D: 3%
49 A: 6% B: 6% C: 88% D: 0%
50 A: 5% B: 7% C: 87% D: 1%
51 A: 11% B: 10% C: 0% D: 79%
52 A: 0% B: 4% C: 15% D: 81%
53 A: 27% B: 0% C: 60% D: 13%
54 A: 0% B: 7% C: 0% D: 93%
55 A: 4% B: 6% C: 11% D: 79%
56 A: 0% B: 84% C: 0% D: 16%
57 A: 33% B: 0% C: 3% D: 64%
58 A: 94% B: 0% C: 6% D: 0%
59 A: 23% B: 13% C: 4% D: 60%
60 A: 0% B: 2% C: 98% D: 0%
61 A: 29% B: 3% C: 2% D: 66%
62 A: 8% B: 5% C: 83% D: 4%
63 A: 0% B: 89% C: 6% D: 5%
64 A: 0% B: 28% C: 5% D: 67%

ASK THE AUDIENCE

£8,000

1	A: 26%	B: 5%	C: 69%	D: 0%
2	A: 9%	B: 4%	C: 9%	D: 78%
3	A: 0%	B: 31%	C: 4%	D: 65%
4	A: 11%	B: 53%	C: 0%	D: 36%
5	A: 2%	B: 0%	C: 0%	D: 98%
6	A: 7%	B: 0%	C: 4%	D: 89%
7	A: 0%	B: 12%	C: 70%	D: 18%
8	A: 87%	B: 8%	C: 0%	D: 5%
9	A: 3%	B: 4%	C: 79%	D: 14%
10	A: 0%	B: 24%	C: 3%	D: 73%
11	A: 27%	B: 0%	C: 73%	D: 0%
12	A: 14%	B: 76%	C: 10%	D: 0%
13	A: 9%	B: 0%	C: 82%	D: 9%
14	A: 97%	B: 3%	C: 0%	D: 0%
15	A: 12%	B: 7%	C: 0%	D: 81%
16	A: 6%	B: 7%	C: 7%	D: 80%
17	A: 4%	B: 23%	C: 59%	D: 14%
18	A: 0%	B: 8%	C: 92%	D: 0%
19	A: 0%	B: 5%	C: 95%	D: 0%
20	A: 0%	B: 94%	C: 6%	D: 0%
21	A: 18%	B: 11%	C: 66%	D: 5%
22	A: 41%	B: 14%	C: 13%	D: 32%
23	A: 0%	B: 0%	C: 90%	D: 10%
24	A: 0%	B: 0%	C: 93%	D: 7%
25	A: 4%	B: 0%	C: 91%	D: 5%
26	A: 9%	B: 0%	C: 81%	D: 10%
27	A: 41%	B: 13%	C: 28%	D: 18%
28	A: 0%	B: 91%	C: 4%	D: 5%
29	A: 8%	B: 0%	C: 4%	D: 88%
30	A: 2%	B: 13%	C: 85%	D: 0%
31	A: 4%	B: 73%	C: 18%	D: 5%
32	A: 5%	B: 82%	C: 8%	D: 5%
33	A: 84%	B: 7%	C: 0%	D: 9%
34	A: 0%	B: 18%	C: 72%	D: 10%
35	A: 4%	B: 16%	C: 0%	D: 80%
36	A: 9%	B: 67%	C: 6%	D: 18%
37	A: 9%	B: 8%	C: 4%	D: 79%
38	A: 19%	B: 75%	C: 0%	D: 6%
39	A: 85%	B: 6%	C: 9%	D: 0%
40	A: 0%	B: 68%	C: 19%	D: 13%
41	A: 51%	B: 13%	C: 4%	D: 32%
42	A: 43%	B: 11%	C: 11%	D: 35%
43	A: 3%	B: 7%	C: 0%	D: 90%
44	A: 59%	B: 4%	C: 5%	D: 32%
45	A: 9%	B: 5%	C: 86%	D: 0%
46	A: 17%	B: 64%	C: 10%	D: 9%
47	A: 97%	B: 0%	C: 3%	D: 0%
48	A: 2%	B: 52%	C: 5%	D: 41%
49	A: 0%	B: 4%	C: 14%	D: 82%
50	A: 0%	B: 5%	C: 87%	D: 8%
51	A: 82%	B: 0%	C: 4%	D: 14%
52	A: 15%	B: 63%	C: 13%	D: 9%
53	A: 6%	B: 86%	C: 8%	D: 0%
54	A: 7%	B: 11%	C: 23%	D: 59%
55	A: 3%	B: 7%	C: 90%	D: 0%
56	A: 0%	B: 0%	C: 7%	D: 93%
57	A: 0%	B: 14%	C: 9%	D: 77%
58	A: 0%	B: 17%	C: 11%	D: 72%
59	A: 13%	B: 79%	C: 8%	D: 0%
60	A: 12%	B: 68%	C: 9%	D: 11%

ASK THE AUDIENCE

£16,000

#	A	B	C	D
1	A: 0%	B: 10%	C: 61%	D: 29%
2	A: 0%	B: 9%	C: 82%	D: 9%
3	A: 33%	B: 51%	C: 12%	D: 4%
4	A: 21%	B: 49%	C: 5%	D: 25%
5	A: 13%	B: 76%	C: 3%	D: 8%
6	A: 12%	B: 53%	C: 22%	D: 13%
7	A: 9%	B: 91%	C: 0%	D: 0%
8	A: 0%	B: 7%	C: 5%	D: 88%
9	A: 6%	B: 0%	C: 77%	D: 17%
10	A: 1%	B: 3%	C: 11%	D: 85%
11	A: 89%	B: 4%	C: 7%	D: 0%
12	A: 58%	B: 0%	C: 24%	D: 18%
13	A: 16%	B: 6%	C: 74%	D: 4%
14	A: 3%	B: 6%	C: 82%	D: 9%
15	A: 0%	B: 85%	C: 0%	D: 15%
16	A: 13%	B: 8%	C: 12%	D: 67%
17	A: 4%	B: 87%	C: 9%	D: 0%
18	A: 7%	B: 20%	C: 48%	D: 25%
19	A: 64%	B: 3%	C: 21%	D: 12%
20	A: 16%	B: 4%	C: 71%	D: 9%
21	A: 0%	B: 79%	C: 6%	D: 15%
22	A: 69%	B: 13%	C: 8%	D: 10%
23	A: 19%	B: 2%	C: 42%	D: 37%
24	A: 3%	B: 24%	C: 72%	D: 1%
25	A: 64%	B: 5%	C: 3%	D: 28%
26	A: 6%	B: 11%	C: 73%	D: 10%
27	A: 0%	B: 0%	C: 9%	D: 91%
28	A: 22%	B: 13%	C: 7%	D: 58%
29	A: 16%	B: 11%	C: 59%	D: 14%
30	A: 15%	B: 71%	C: 13%	D: 1%
31	A: 79%	B: 7%	C: 9%	D: 5%
32	A: 51%	B: 6%	C: 18%	D: 25%
33	A: 3%	B: 23%	C: 68%	D: 6%
34	A: 0%	B: 26%	C: 66%	D: 8%
35	A: 0%	B: 0%	C: 89%	D: 11%
36	A: 4%	B: 63%	C: 29%	D: 4%
37	A: 12%	B: 79%	C: 0%	D: 9%
38	A: 28%	B: 59%	C: 0%	D: 13%
39	A: 17%	B: 40%	C: 13%	D: 30%
40	A: 9%	B: 0%	C: 25%	D: 66%
41	A: 14%	B: 54%	C: 20%	D: 12%
42	A: 15%	B: 0%	C: 18%	D: 67%
43	A: 7%	B: 0%	C: 9%	D: 84%
44	A: 64%	B: 3%	C: 21%	D: 12%
45	A: 76%	B: 11%	C: 13%	D: 0%
46	A: 12%	B: 13%	C: 55%	D: 20%
47	A: 4%	B: 0%	C: 21%	D: 75%
48	A: 9%	B: 8%	C: 66%	D: 17%
49	A: 0%	B: 28%	C: 67%	D: 5%
50	A: 72%	B: 0%	C: 7%	D: 21%
51	A: 33%	B: 34%	C: 29%	D: 4%
52	A: 59%	B: 13%	C: 19%	D: 9%
53	A: 8%	B: 79%	C: 0%	D: 13%
54	A: 5%	B: 20%	C: 75%	D: 0%
55	A: 3%	B: 89%	C: 8%	D: 0%
56	A: 32%	B: 68%	C: 0%	D: 0%

ASK THE AUDIENCE

£32,000

1	A: 60%	B: 7%	C: 19%	D: 14%
2	A: 36%	B: 53%	C: 4%	D: 7%
3	A: 22%	B: 12%	C: 8%	D: 58%
4	A: 9%	B: 13%	C: 78%	D: 0%
5	A: 43%	B: 27%	C: 6%	D: 24%
6	A: 30%	B: 62%	C: 0%	D: 8%
7	A: 6%	B: 51%	C: 20%	D: 23%
8	A: 5%	B: 10%	C: 29%	D: 56%
9	A: 10%	B: 15%	C: 61%	D: 14%
10	A: 17%	B: 72%	C: 11%	D: 0%
11	A: 35%	B: 30%	C: 35%	D: 0%
12	A: 19%	B: 2%	C: 20%	D: 59%
13	A: 0%	B: 21%	C: 64%	D: 15%
14	A: 7%	B: 0%	C: 93%	D: 0%
15	A: 31%	B: 7%	C: 12%	D: 50%
16	A: 0%	B: 75%	C: 6%	D: 19%
17	A: 66%	B: 21%	C: 13%	D: 0%
18	A: 71%	B: 10%	C: 19%	D: 0%
19	A: 57%	B: 33%	C: 10%	D: 0%
20	A: 50%	B: 9%	C: 9%	D: 32%
21	A: 92%	B: 0%	C: 8%	D: 0%
22	A: 5%	B: 16%	C: 79%	D: 0%
23	A: 0%	B: 71%	C: 4%	D: 25%
24	A: 21%	B: 0%	C: 43%	D: 36%
25	A: 0%	B: 62%	C: 38%	D: 0%
26	A: 88%	B: 0%	C: 0%	D: 12%
27	A: 8%	B: 92%	C: 0%	D: 0%
28	A: 36%	B: 29%	C: 14%	D: 21%
29	A: 69%	B: 15%	C: 1%	D: 15%
30	A: 43%	B: 57%	C: 0%	D: 0%
31	A: 0%	B: 79%	C: 21%	D: 0%
32	A: 50%	B: 34%	C: 7%	D: 9%
33	A: 3%	B: 28%	C: 69%	D: 0%
34	A: 5%	B: 23%	C: 72%	D: 0%
35	A: 65%	B: 16%	C: 6%	D: 13%
36	A: 19%	B: 12%	C: 0%	D: 69%
37	A: 0%	B: 2%	C: 25%	D: 73%
38	A: 24%	B: 0%	C: 72%	D: 4%
39	A: 13%	B: 22%	C: 8%	D: 57%
40	A: 43%	B: 0%	C: 43%	D: 14%
41	A: 36%	B: 0%	C: 23%	D: 41%
42	A: 31%	B: 69%	C: 0%	D: 0%
43	A: 0%	B: 39%	C: 9%	D: 52%
44	A: 0%	B: 48%	C: 30%	D: 22%
45	A: 21%	B: 37%	C: 20%	D: 22%
46	A: 28%	B: 0%	C: 14%	D: 58%
47	A: 29%	B: 0%	C: 71%	D: 0%
48	A: 6%	B: 34%	C: 60%	D: 0%
49	A: 0%	B: 13%	C: 24%	D: 63%
50	A: 36%	B: 13%	C: 15%	D: 36%
51	A: 29%	B: 47%	C: 3%	D: 21%
52	A: 30%	B: 43%	C: 13%	D: 14%

ASK THE AUDIENCE

£64,000

1	A: 71%	B: 4%	C: 20%	D: 5%
2	A: 23%	B: 0%	C: 50%	D: 27%
3	A: 4%	B: 55%	C: 22%	D: 19%
4	A: 16%	B: 15%	C: 42%	D: 27%
5	A: 48%	B: 32%	C: 10%	D: 10%
6	A: 59%	B: 36%	C: 5%	D: 0%
7	A: 9%	B: 82%	C: 9%	D: 0%
8	A: 13%	B: 31%	C: 29%	D: 27%
9	A: 2%	B: 71%	C: 20%	D: 7%
10	A: 18%	B: 54%	C: 15%	D: 13%
11	A: 19%	B: 0%	C: 5%	D: 76%
12	A: 64%	B: 14%	C: 9%	D: 13%
13	A: 68%	B: 0%	C: 5%	D: 27%
14	A: 44%	B: 15%	C: 0%	D: 41%
15	A: 11%	B: 84%	C: 0%	D: 5%
16	A: 0%	B: 4%	C: 23%	D: 73%
17	A: 59%	B: 19%	C: 13%	D: 9%
18	A: 5%	B: 4%	C: 27%	D: 64%
19	A: 76%	B: 3%	C: 6%	D: 15%
20	A: 45%	B: 36%	C: 5%	D: 14%
21	A: 46%	B: 28%	C: 26%	D: 0%
22	A: 86%	B: 9%	C: 5%	D: 0%
23	A: 73%	B: 0%	C: 0%	D: 27%
24	A: 23%	B: 41%	C: 34%	D: 2%
25	A: 0%	B: 24%	C: 7%	D: 69%
26	A: 10%	B: 0%	C: 72%	D: 18%
27	A: 0%	B: 4%	C: 81%	D: 15%
28	A: 9%	B: 91%	C: 0%	D: 0%
29	A: 5%	B: 11%	C: 0%	D: 84%
30	A: 8%	B: 0%	C: 83%	D: 9%
31	A: 0%	B: 23%	C: 4%	D: 73%
32	A: 12%	B: 26%	C: 55%	D: 7%
33	A: 87%	B: 13%	C: 0%	D: 0%
34	A: 0%	B: 12%	C: 0%	D: 88%
35	A: 77%	B: 8%	C: 15%	D: 0%
36	A: 14%	B: 80%	C: 1%	D: 5%
37	A: 79%	B: 3%	C: 11%	D: 7%
38	A: 15%	B: 81%	C: 0%	D: 4%
39	A: 6%	B: 90%	C: 4%	D: 0%
40	A: 10%	B: 0%	C: 18%	D: 72%
41	A: 9%	B: 23%	C: 27%	D: 41%
42	A: 19%	B: 64%	C: 5%	D: 12%
43	A: 59%	B: 22%	C: 5%	D: 14%
44	A: 67%	B: 10%	C: 8%	D: 15%
45	A: 61%	B: 25%	C: 3%	D: 11%
46	A: 14%	B: 4%	C: 63%	D: 19%
47	A: 11%	B: 13%	C: 38%	D: 38%
48	A: 21%	B: 2%	C: 61%	D: 16%

ASK THE AUDIENCE

£125,000

1	A: 30%	B: 5%	C: 12%	D: 53%
2	A: 62%	B: 11%	C: 17%	D: 10%
3	A: 67%	B: 15%	C: 10%	D: 8%
4	A: 29%	B: 21%	C: 19%	D: 31%
5	A: 63%	B: 0%	C: 25%	D: 12%
6	A: 3%	B: 26%	C: 10%	D: 61%
7	A: 59%	B: 24%	C: 13%	D: 4%
8	A: 54%	B: 12%	C: 13%	D: 21%
9	A: 38%	B: 10%	C: 46%	D: 6%
10	A: 52%	B: 21%	C: 27%	D: 0%
11	A: 50%	B: 23%	C: 19%	D: 8%
12	A: 15%	B: 2%	C: 79%	D: 4%
13	A: 7%	B: 79%	C: 9%	D: 5%
14	A: 8%	B: 54%	C: 13%	D: 25%
15	A: 13%	B: 81%	C: 0%	D: 6%
16	A: 21%	B: 49%	C: 21%	D: 9%
17	A: 0%	B: 23%	C: 65%	D: 12%
18	A: 12%	B: 13%	C: 20%	D: 55%
19	A: 8%	B: 17%	C: 62%	D: 13%
20	A: 79%	B: 10%	C: 0%	D: 11%
21	A: 46%	B: 0%	C: 8%	D: 46%
22	A: 8%	B: 17%	C: 25%	D: 50%
23	A: 37%	B: 4%	C: 34%	D: 25%
24	A: 2%	B: 65%	C: 33%	D: 0%
25	A: 15%	B: 31%	C: 42%	D: 12%
26	A: 24%	B: 29%	C: 29%	D: 18%
27	A: 19%	B: 0%	C: 0%	D: 81%
28	A: 21%	B: 0%	C: 75%	D: 4%
29	A: 22%	B: 4%	C: 70%	D: 4%
30	A: 21%	B: 54%	C: 17%	D: 8%
31	A: 9%	B: 74%	C: 4%	D: 13%
32	A: 38%	B: 4%	C: 33%	D: 25%
33	A: 32%	B: 8%	C: 54%	D: 6%
34	A: 42%	B: 11%	C: 27%	D: 20%
35	A: 9%	B: 31%	C: 18%	D: 42%
36	A: 36%	B: 22%	C: 4%	D: 38%
37	A: 19%	B: 27%	C: 43%	D: 11%
38	A: 21%	B: 50%	C: 25%	D: 4%
39	A: 79%	B: 5%	C: 4%	D: 12%
40	A: 14%	B: 33%	C: 33%	D: 20%
41	A: 36%	B: 7%	C: 32%	D: 25%
42	A: 49%	B: 22%	C: 0%	D: 29%
43	A: 19%	B: 24%	C: 7%	D: 50%
44	A: 5%	B: 19%	C: 34%	D: 42%

ASK THE AUDIENCE

£250,000

1	A: 68%	B: 27%	C: 5%	D: 0%
2	A: 18%	B: 0%	C: 17%	D: 65%
3	A: 64%	B: 16%	C: 16%	D: 4%
4	A: 2%	B: 0%	C: 32%	D: 66%
5	A: 41%	B: 45%	C: 5%	D: 9%
6	A: 10%	B: 4%	C: 5%	D: 81%
7	A: 95%	B: 5%	C: 0%	D: 0%
8	A: 3%	B: 15%	C: 23%	D: 59%
9	A: 8%	B: 77%	C: 14%	D: 1%
10	A: 2%	B: 7%	C: 86%	D: 5%
11	A: 0%	B: 80%	C: 10%	D: 10%
12	A: 0%	B: 9%	C: 91%	D: 0%
13	A: 23%	B: 18%	C: 36%	D: 23%
14	A: 0%	B: 43%	C: 32%	D: 25%
15	A: 14%	B: 0%	C: 14%	D: 72%
16	A: 41%	B: 27%	C: 8%	D: 24%
17	A: 59%	B: 0%	C: 5%	D: 36%
18	A: 50%	B: 35%	C: 10%	D: 5%
19	A: 85%	B: 8%	C: 3%	D: 4%
20	A: 39%	B: 20%	C: 18%	D: 23%
21	A: 51%	B: 17%	C: 14%	D: 18%
22	A: 21%	B: 18%	C: 16%	D: 45%
23	A: 5%	B: 33%	C: 26%	D: 36%
24	A: 13%	B: 15%	C: 31%	D: 41%
25	A: 4%	B: 5%	C: 62%	D: 29%
26	A: 9%	B: 24%	C: 40%	D: 27%
27	A: 10%	B: 44%	C: 19%	D: 27%
28	A: 82%	B: 13%	C: 1%	D: 4%
29	A: 15%	B: 32%	C: 44%	D: 9%
30	A: 20%	B: 12%	C: 68%	D: 0%
31	A: 4%	B: 5%	C: 18%	D: 73%
32	A: 59%	B: 27%	C: 9%	D: 5%
33	A: 23%	B: 45%	C: 19%	D: 13%
34	A: 13%	B: 10%	C: 59%	D: 18%
35	A: 4%	B: 0%	C: 91%	D: 5%
36	A: 24%	B: 73%	C: 0%	D: 3%
37	A: 41%	B: 0%	C: 16%	D: 43%
38	A: 25%	B: 52%	C: 15%	D: 8%
39	A: 14%	B: 23%	C: 16%	D: 47%
40	A: 20%	B: 5%	C: 34%	D: 41%

£500,000

1	A: 13%	B: 4%	C: 50%	D: 33%
2	A: 15%	B: 19%	C: 39%	D: 27%
3	A: 11%	B: 55%	C: 6%	D: 28%
4	A: 25%	B: 3%	C: 33%	D: 39%
5	A: 13%	B: 2%	C: 85%	D: 0%
6	A: 7%	B: 23%	C: 29%	D: 41%
7	A: 5%	B: 61%	C: 16%	D: 18%
8	A: 17%	B: 66%	C: 4%	D: 13%
9	A: 11%	B: 8%	C: 9%	D: 72%
10	A: 44%	B: 12%	C: 0%	D: 44%
11	A: 12%	B: 45%	C: 18%	D: 25%
12	A: 22%	B: 0%	C: 50%	D: 28%
13	A: 7%	B: 51%	C: 9%	D: 33%
14	A: 22%	B: 67%	C: 6%	D: 5%
15	A: 11%	B: 19%	C: 55%	D: 15%
16	A: 14%	B: 28%	C: 35%	D: 23%
17	A: 30%	B: 43%	C: 27%	D: 0%
18	A: 39%	B: 31%	C: 28%	D: 2%
19	A: 3%	B: 47%	C: 41%	D: 9%
20	A: 15%	B: 19%	C: 37%	D: 29%
21	A: 19%	B: 8%	C: 6%	D: 67%
22	A: 0%	B: 23%	C: 77%	D: 0%
23	A: 82%	B: 0%	C: 18%	D: 0%
24	A: 20%	B: 61%	C: 5%	D: 14%
25	A: 10%	B: 33%	C: 53%	D: 4%
26	A: 22%	B: 32%	C: 7%	D: 39%
27	A: 0%	B: 14%	C: 83%	D: 3%
28	A: 19%	B: 28%	C: 16%	D: 37%
29	A: 6%	B: 43%	C: 12%	D: 39%
30	A: 10%	B: 47%	C: 8%	D: 35%
31	A: 24%	B: 39%	C: 4%	D: 33%
32	A: 61%	B: 5%	C: 6%	D: 28%
33	A: 23%	B: 12%	C: 42%	D: 23%
34	A: 0%	B: 82%	C: 11%	D: 7%
35	A: 62%	B: 25%	C: 13%	D: 0%
36	A: 7%	B: 26%	C: 33%	D: 34%

ASK THE AUDIENCE

£1,000,000

1	A: 24%	B: 71%	C: 0%	D: 5%
2	A: 54%	B: 25%	C: 13%	D: 8%
3	A: 47%	B: 22%	C: 31%	D: 0%
4	A: 0%	B: 57%	C: 9%	D: 34%
5	A: 46%	B: 21%	C: 21%	D: 12%
6	A: 19%	B: 50%	C: 12%	D: 19%
7	A: 7%	B: 13%	C: 18%	D: 62%
8	A: 38%	B: 33%	C: 6%	D: 23%
9	A: 32%	B: 59%	C: 5%	D: 4%
10	A: 18%	B: 3%	C: 54%	D: 25%
11	A: 42%	B: 16%	C: 42%	D: 0%
12	A: 19%	B: 4%	C: 12%	D: 65%
13	A: 11%	B: 46%	C: 29%	D: 14%
14	A: 67%	B: 6%	C: 21%	D: 6%
15	A: 23%	B: 32%	C: 29%	D: 16%
16	A: 0%	B: 38%	C: 33%	D: 29%
17	A: 25%	B: 20%	C: 37%	D: 18%
18	A: 35%	B: 36%	C: 21%	D: 8%
19	A: 18%	B: 15%	C: 42%	D: 25%
20	A: 24%	B: 30%	C: 0%	D: 46%
21	A: 40%	B: 29%	C: 14%	D: 17%
22	A: 0%	B: 43%	C: 38%	D: 19%
23	A: 67%	B: 25%	C: 8%	D: 0%
24	A: 45%	B: 29%	C: 12%	D: 14%
25	A: 49%	B: 34%	C: 7%	D: 10%
26	A: 9%	B: 28%	C: 63%	D: 0%
27	A: 12%	B: 27%	C: 56%	D: 5%
28	A: 59%	B: 2%	C: 37%	D: 2%
29	A: 3%	B: 26%	C: 13%	D: 58%
30	A: 13%	B: 25%	C: 44%	D: 18%
31	A: 2%	B: 0%	C: 63%	D: 35%
32	A: 29%	B: 11%	C: 60%	D: 0%

Answers

Fastest Finger First

1	BDAC	2	DACB	3	DACB	4	ACDB	5	DBAC
6	DBAC	7	BCDA	8	CADB	9	DABC	10	CBDA
11	DBAC	12	BDAC	13	ACBD	14	ADCB	15	ABCD
16	ACBD	17	DACB	18	BACD	19	ADCB	20	DCBA
21	BACD	22	DCAB	23	CBDA	24	CABD	25	CABD
26	BACD	27	DBAC	28	ABCD	29	BDAC	30	DBAC
31	DACB	32	CBDA	33	CABD	34	DCBA	35	CADB
36	BADC	37	CABD	38	DABC	39	CADB	40	BDCA
41	CBAD	42	BACD	43	DCBA	44	ADCB	45	ABCD
46	CBDA	47	CABD	48	ACDB	49	ACDB	50	CABD
51	BDAC	52	BDAC	53	DBAC	54	CADB	55	BCDA
56	CABD	57	CADB	58	BDCA	59	CBDA	60	DACB
61	BACD	62	DCAB	63	CADB	64	DCAB	65	BACD
66	CDAB	67	CADB	68	DACB	69	CADB	70	CBAD
71	BACD	72	CDAB	73	DACB	74	CADB	75	BDCA
76	DBAC	77	CBDA	78	DBAC	79	CBAD	80	ADCB
81	BCAD	82	DACB	83	BCDA	84	CBAD	85	DBCA
86	BACD	87	DABC	88	DBAC	89	BADC	90	DCAB
91	DABC	92	CDAB	93	DCAB	94	CDAB	95	BCAD
96	CBAD	97	CBDA	98	CDAB	99	CDBA	100	CADB

If you answered correctly, well done! Turn to page 31 to play for £100!

£100

1	B	2	C	3	D	4	C	5	D
6	B	7	B	8	B	9	A	10	A
11	D	12	B	13	B	14	C	15	A
16	C	17	A	18	C	19	B	20	D
21	A	22	D	23	C	24	A	25	D
26	B	27	C	28	C	29	A	30	C
31	A	32	B	33	A	34	B	35	C
36	D	37	B	38	B	39	B	40	D
41	B	42	B	43	A	44	B	45	A
46	A	47	B	48	C	49	C	50	B
51	A	52	B	53	A	54	B	55	B
56	C	57	B	58	C	59	A	60	B
61	A	62	B	63	B	64	A	65	B
66	C	67	A	68	B	69	A	70	C

ANSWERS

71 A	72 B	73 C	74 B	75 B
76 C	77 B	78 A	79 C	80 D
81 C	82 A	83 B	84 A	85 A
86 B	87 A	88 A		

If you have won £100, well done! Turn to page 51 to play for £200!

£200

1 A	2 C	3 C	4 A	5 C
6 D	7 A	8 C	9 C	10 B
11 C	12 C	13 A	14 D	15 C
16 B	17 C	18 C	19 C	20 B
21 B	22 C	23 C	24 A	25 B
26 B	27 C	28 C	29 A	30 C
31 D	32 B	33 C	34 B	35 B
36 D	37 A	38 D	39 C	40 B
41 A	42 C	43 B	44 B	45 D
46 C	47 B	48 B	49 C	50 A
51 B	52 B	53 B	54 D	55 D
56 D	57 B	58 A	59 C	60 B
61 C	62 C	63 D	64 A	65 C
66 A	67 D	68 A	69 D	70 B
71 C	72 D	73 B	74 A	75 C
76 D	77 C	78 B	79 A	80 C
81 D	82 A	83 B	84 C	

If you have won £200, well done! Turn to page 69 to play for £300!

£300

1 D	2 D	3 C	4 B	5 D
6 D	7 C	8 C	9 D	10 B
11 C	12 C	13 C	14 C	15 A
16 B	17 D	18 C	19 B	20 B
21 C	22 D	23 A	24 D	25 B
26 C	27 D	28 A	29 D	30 C
31 A	32 D	33 D	34 A	35 B
36 B	37 B	38 D	39 C	40 C
41 D	42 D	43 C	44 C	45 B
46 B	47 C	48 C	49 C	50 C
51 C	52 B	53 D	54 C	55 C
56 A	57 B	58 D	59 A	60 C
61 D	62 A	63 C	64 D	65 C
66 C	67 D	68 C	69 C	70 B
71 B	72 D	73 D	74 C	75 C
76 C	77 B	78 A	79 D	80 A

If you have won £300, well done! Turn to page 87 to play for £500!

ANSWERS

£500

1 D	2 C	3 C	4 B	5 A
6 C	7 C	8 C	9 D	10 C
11 B	12 D	13 A	14 C	15 C
16 A	17 D	18 C	19 D	20 C
21 A	22 C	23 D	24 B	25 B
26 D	27 A	28 B	29 C	30 D
31 B	32 A	33 B	34 A	35 C
36 B	37 A	38 C	39 C	40 B
41 C	42 C	43 D	44 D	45 C
46 D	47 A	48 B	49 A	50 A
51 B	52 C	53 A	54 A	55 A
56 B	57 D	58 A	59 B	60 B
61 D	62 B	63 A	64 C	65 C
66 B	67 C	68 B	69 B	70 B
71 A	72 A	73 D	74 D	75 B
76 B				

If you have won £500, well done! Turn to page 105 to play for £1,000!

£1,000

1 B	2 C	3 C	4 D	5 C
6 A	7 B	8 A	9 C	10 C
11 A	12 A	13 B	14 D	15 C
16 B	17 A	18 C	19 C	20 A
21 B	22 C	23 D	24 B	25 D
26 B	27 D	28 B	29 A	30 A
31 C	32 B	33 D	34 D	35 D
36 C	37 C	38 B	39 D	40 B
41 D	42 C	43 B	44 C	45 A
46 B	47 D	48 C	49 D	50 A
51 C	52 A	53 A	54 D	55 C
56 C	57 C	58 A	59 A	60 C
61 B	62 A	63 B	64 C	65 C
66 D	67 B	68 A	69 D	70 B
71 C	72 B			

If you have won £1,000, well done! Turn to page 121 to play for £2,000!

£2,000

1 A	2 C	3 A	4 C	5 C
6 C	7 C	8 C	9 A	10 A
11 B	12 D	13 C	14 C	15 A
16 A	17 C	18 A	19 B	20 C
21 B	22 D	23 D	24 D	25 B

ANSWERS

26	B	27	C	28	C	29	D	30	C
31	B	32	A	33	D	34	A	35	C
36	A	37	A	38	D	39	C	40	A
41	B	42	D	43	D	44	D	45	C
46	C	47	A	48	A	49	D	50	D
51	C	52	C	53	C	54	A	55	A
56	D	57	B	58	B	59	A	60	C
61	A	62	B	63	C	64	A	65	C
66	A	67	B	68	D				

If you have won £2,000, well done! Turn to page 137 to play for £4,000!

£4,000

1	B	2	D	3	C	4	A	5	C
6	B	7	D	8	C	9	B	10	B
11	D	12	A	13	A	14	A	15	C
16	D	17	B	18	A	19	A	20	B
21	B	22	C	23	B	24	B	25	A
26	D	27	D	28	B	29	B	30	C
31	C	32	C	33	A	34	B	35	A
36	B	37	D	38	B	39	C	40	A
41	B	42	D	43	D	44	D	45	C
46	B	47	B	48	C	49	C	50	C
51	D	52	D	53	C	54	D	55	D
56	B	57	D	58	A	59	D	60	C
61	D	62	C	63	B	64	D		

If you have won £4,000, well done! Turn to page 151 to play for £8,000!

£8,000

1	C	2	D	3	D	4	B	5	D
6	D	7	C	8	A	9	C	10	D
11	C	12	B	13	C	14	A	15	D
16	D	17	C	18	C	19	C	20	B
21	B	22	D	23	C	24	C	25	C
26	C	27	A	28	B	29	D	30	C
31	B	32	B	33	A	34	C	35	D
36	B	37	D	38	B	39	B	40	B
41	D	42	A	43	D	44	A	45	C
46	B	47	A	48	D	49	D	50	C
51	A	52	B	53	B	54	D	55	C
56	D	57	D	58	D	59	B	60	B

If you have won £8,000, well done! Turn to page 165 to play for £16,000!

ANSWERS

£16,000

1	C	2	C	3	A	4	B	5	B
6	B	7	B	8	D	9	C	10	D
11	A	12	A	13	C	14	C	15	B
16	D	17	B	18	C	19	A	20	C
21	B	22	A	23	C	24	C	25	A
26	C	27	D	28	D	29	C	30	B
31	A	32	A	33	C	34	C	35	C
36	B	37	B	38	B	39	B	40	D
41	B	42	D	43	D	44	A	45	A
46	C	47	D	48	C	49	C	50	A
51	B	52	A	53	B	54	C	55	B
56	B								

If you have won £16,000, well done! Turn to page 179 to play for £32,000!

£32,000

1	A	2	B	3	D	4	C	5	A
6	B	7	B	8	D	9	C	10	B
11	B	12	D	13	C	14	C	15	D
16	B	17	A	18	A	19	A	20	D
21	A	22	C	23	C	24	D	25	B
26	A	27	B	28	A	29	A	30	A
31	B	32	A	33	C	34	C	35	A
36	D	37	D	38	C	39	D	40	C
41	D	42	B	43	D	44	D	45	A
46	C	47	C	48	B	49	D	50	B
51	B	52	A						

If you have won £32,000, well done! Turn to page 191 to play for £64,000!

£64,000

1	A	2	C	3	B	4	C	5	A
6	A	7	B	8	A	9	B	10	B
11	D	12	A	13	A	14	A	15	B
16	D	17	A	18	D	19	A	20	A
21	B	22	A	23	A	24	B	25	D
26	C	27	C	28	B	29	D	30	C
31	D	32	C	33	A	34	D	35	A
36	B	37	A	38	B	39	B	40	D
41	D	42	B	43	A	44	A	45	A
46	C	47	D	48	C					

If you have won £64,000, well done! Turn to page 203 to play for £125,000!

ANSWERS

£125,000

1	D	2	A	3	A	4	D	5	C
6	D	7	A	8	A	9	A	10	B
11	A	12	C	13	B	14	B	15	B
16	B	17	C	18	D	19	C	20	A
21	D	22	A	23	A	24	B	25	C
26	C	27	D	28	C	29	C	30	B
31	B	32	D	33	C	34	A	35	D
36	A	37	B	38	B	39	A	40	B
41	D	42	A	43	D	44	D		

If you have won £125,000, well done! Turn to page 213 to play for £250,000!

£250,000

1	A	2	D	3	A	4	D	5	B
6	D	7	A	8	D	9	B	10	C
11	B	12	C	13	A	14	B	15	D
16	A	17	A	18	B	19	A	20	A
21	A	22	D	23	B	24	D	25	C
26	C	27	B	28	A	29	B	30	C
31	D	32	A	33	B	34	C	35	C
36	B	37	D	38	B	39	D	40	C

If you have won £250,000, well done! Turn to page 223 to play for £500,000!

£500,000

1	D	2	C	3	A	4	D	5	C
6	D	7	B	8	B	9	D	10	D
11	D	12	C	13	B	14	B	15	D
16	C	17	C	18	C	19	C	20	A
21	D	22	A	23	A	24	B	25	B
26	B	27	C	28	B	29	B	30	B
31	B	32	A	33	B	34	B	35	C
36	C								

If you have won £500,000, well done! Turn to page 233 to play for £1,000,000!

£1,000,000

1	B	2	A	3	B	4	B	5	A
6	A	7	B	8	A	9	B	10	C
11	A	12	A	13	B	14	A	15	C
16	C	17	C	18	C	19	C	20	D
21	C	22	B	23	D	24	C	25	B
26	C	27	B	28	C	29	D	30	B
31	C	32	C						

If you have won £1,000,000, well done! You're a millionaire!

Score sheets

Write your name and the names of any other contestants in the space provided. Shade in each of the boxes lightly with a pencil once you or one of your fellow contestants has won the amount in that box. If you or any of the other contestants answer a question incorrectly and are out of the game, use a soft eraser to rub out the relevant boxes so that the final score is showing.

S C O R E   S H E E T

contestant's name	contestant's name
....	....

15	£1 MILLION	15	£1 MILLION
14	£500,000	14	£500,000
13	£250,000	13	£250,000
12	£125,000	12	£125,000
11	£64,000	11	£64,000
10	£32,000	10	£32,000
9	£16,000	9	£16,000
8	£8,000	8	£8,000
7	£4,000	7	£4,000
6	£2,000	6	£2,000
5	£1,000	5	£1,000
4	£500	4	£500
3	£300	3	£300
2	£200	2	£200
1	£100	1	£100

S C O R E   S H E E T

contestant's name	contestant's name
....	....

50:50	👥	☎	50:50	👥	☎
☐	☐	☐	☐	☐	☐

15	£1 MILLION	15	£1 MILLION
14	£500,000	14	£500,000
13	£250,000	13	£250,000
12	£125,000	12	£125,000
11	£64,000	11	£64,000
10	£32,000	10	£32,000
9	£16,000	9	£16,000
8	£8,000	8	£8,000
7	£4,000	7	£4,000
6	£2,000	6	£2,000
5	£1,000	5	£1,000
4	£500	4	£500
3	£300	3	£300
2	£200	2	£200
1	£100	1	£100

SCORE SHEET

contestant's name	contestant's name
....	....

50:50	👥	☎		50:50	👥	☎
☐	☐	☐		☐	☐	☐

15	£1 MILLION	15	£1 MILLION
14	£500,000	14	£500,000
13	£250,000	13	£250,000
12	£125,000	12	£125,000
11	£64,000	11	£64,000
10	£32,000	**10**	£32,000
9	£16,000	9	£16,000
8	£8,000	8	£8,000
7	£4,000	7	£4,000
6	£2,000	6	£2,000
5	£1,000	**5**	£1,000
4	£500	4	£500
3	£300	3	£300
2	£200	2	£200
1	£100	1	£100

SCORE SHEET

contestant's name		contestant's name	
....		....	

50:50	👥	📞		50:50	👥	📞
☐	☐	☐		☐	☐	☐

15	£1 MILLION		15	£1 MILLION
14	£500,000		14	£500,000
13	£250,000		13	£250,000
12	£125,000		12	£125,000
11	£64,000		11	£64,000
10	£32,000		10	£32,000
9	£16,000		9	£16,000
8	£8,000		8	£8,000
7	£4,000		7	£4,000
6	£2,000		6	£2,000
5	£1,000		5	£1,000
4	£500		4	£500
3	£300		3	£300
2	£200		2	£200
1	£100		1	£100

S C O R E   S H E E T

contestant's name

....

50:50 · 👥 · ☎
▢ ▢ ▢

15	£1 MILLION
14	£500,000
13	£250,000
12	£125,000
11	£64,000
10	£32,000
9	£16,000
8	£8,000
7	£4,000
6	£2,000
5	£1,000
4	£500
3	£300
2	£200
1	£100

contestant's name

....

50:50 · 👥 · ☎
▢ ▢ ▢

15	£1 MILLION
14	£500,000
13	£250,000
12	£125,000
11	£64,000
10	£32,000
9	£16,000
8	£8,000
7	£4,000
6	£2,000
5	£1,000
4	£500
3	£300
2	£200
1	£100

SCORE SHEET

....

50:50 👥 ☎

☐ ☐ ☐

15	£1 MILLION
14	£500,000
13	£250,000
12	£125,000
11	£64,000
10	£32,000
9	£16,000
8	£8,000
7	£4,000
6	£2,000
5	£1,000
4	£500
3	£300
2	£200
1	£100

....

50:50 👥 ☎

☐ ☐ ☐

15	£1 MILLION
14	£500,000
13	£250,000
12	£125,000
11	£64,000
10	£32,000
9	£16,000
8	£8,000
7	£4,000
6	£2,000
5	£1,000
4	£500
3	£300
2	£200
1	£100

SCORE SHEET

contestant's name

....

☐   ☐   ☐

15	£1 MILLION
14	£500,000
13	£250,000
12	£125,000
11	£64,000
10	£32,000
9	£16,000
8	£8,000
7	£4,000
6	£2,000
5	£1,000
4	£500
3	£300
2	£200
1	£100

contestant's name

....

☐   ☐   ☐

15	£1 MILLION
14	£500,000
13	£250,000
12	£125,000
11	£64,000
10	£32,000
9	£16,000
8	£8,000
7	£4,000
6	£2,000
5	£1,000
4	£500
3	£300
2	£200
1	£100

SCORE SHEET

contestant's name		contestant's name
....		....

50:50 👥 📞   **50:50** 👥 📞

☐ ☐ ☐   ☐ ☐ ☐

15	£1 MILLION		15	£1 MILLION
14	£500,000		14	£500,000
13	£250,000		13	£250,000
12	£125,000		12	£125,000
11	£64,000		11	£64,000
10	£32,000		**10**	£32,000
9	£16,000		9	£16,000
8	£8,000		8	£8,000
7	£4,000		7	£4,000
6	£2,000		6	£2,000
5	£1,000		**5**	£1,000
4	£500		4	£500
3	£300		3	£300
2	£200		2	£200
1	£100		1	£100

SCORE SHEET

contestant's name	contestant's name
....	....

50:50	👥	☎		50:50	👥	☎
☐	☐	☐		☐	☐	☐

15	£1 MILLION		15	£1 MILLION
14	£500,000		14	£500,000
13	£250,000		13	£250,000
12	£125,000		12	£125,000
11	£64,000		11	£64,000
10	£32,000		10	£32,000
9	£16,000		9	£16,000
8	£8,000		8	£8,000
7	£4,000		7	£4,000
6	£2,000		6	£2,000
5	£1,000		5	£1,000
4	£500		4	£500
3	£300		3	£300
2	£200		2	£200
1	£100		1	£100

SCORE SHEET

50:50	👥	📞
☐	☐	☐

15	£1 MILLION
14	£500,000
13	£250,000
12	£125,000
11	£64,000
10	£32,000
9	£16,000
8	£8,000
7	£4,000
6	£2,000
5	£1,000
4	£500
3	£300
2	£200
1	£100

50:50	👥	📞
☐	☐	☐

15	£1 MILLION
14	£500,000
13	£250,000
12	£125,000
11	£64,000
10	£32,000
9	£16,000
8	£8,000
7	£4,000
6	£2,000
5	£1,000
4	£500
3	£300
2	£200
1	£100

SCORE SHEET

....

50:50

....

50:50

15	£1 MILLION	15	£1 MILLION
14	£500,000	14	£500,000
13	£250,000	13	£250,000
12	£125,000	12	£125,000
11	£64,000	11	£64,000
10	£32,000	10	£32,000
9	£16,000	9	£16,000
8	£8,000	8	£8,000
7	£4,000	7	£4,000
6	£2,000	6	£2,000
5	£1,000	5	£1,000
4	£500	4	£500
3	£300	3	£300
2	£200	2	£200
1	£100	1	£100

SCORE SHEET

contestant's name	contestant's name
....	....

50:50	👥	☎	50:50	👥	☎
☐	☐	☐	☐	☐	☐

15	£1 MILLION	15	£1 MILLION
14	£500,000	14	£500,000
13	£250,000	13	£250,000
12	£125,000	12	£125,000
11	£64,000	11	£64,000
10	£32,000	**10**	£32,000
9	£16,000	9	£16,000
8	£8,000	8	£8,000
7	£4,000	7	£4,000
6	£2,000	6	£2,000
5	£1,000	**5**	£1,000
4	£500	4	£500
3	£300	3	£300
2	£200	2	£200
1	£100	1	£100

S C O R E   S H E E T

50:50

15	£1 MILLION
14	£500,000
13	£250,000
12	£125,000
11	£64,000
10	£32,000
9	£16,000
8	£8,000
7	£4,000
6	£2,000
5	£1,000
4	£500
3	£300
2	£200
1	£100

50:50

15	£1 MILLION
14	£500,000
13	£250,000
12	£125,000
11	£64,000
10	£32,000
9	£16,000
8	£8,000
7	£4,000
6	£2,000
5	£1,000
4	£500
3	£300
2	£200
1	£100